HOW TO
ADOPT A
CHILD

A COMPREHENSIVE GUIDE
FOR PROSPECTIVE PARENTS

HOW TO ADOPT A CHILD

A COMPREHENSIVE GUIDE FOR PROSPECTIVE PARENTS

Connie Crain

Janice Duffy

Publishers since 1798

Thomas Nelson Publishers
Nashville • Atlanta • London • Vancouver

Published in Nashville, Tennessee, by Thomas Nelson, Inc., Publishers, and distributed in Canada by Word Communications, Ltd., Richmond, British Columbia, and in the United Kingdom by Word (UK), Ltd., Milton Keynes, England.

Library of Congress Cataloging-in-Publication Data

Crain, Connie.
    How to adopt a child: a comprehensive guide for prospective parents / Connie Crain and Janice Duffy.
        p.   cm.
    Includes bibliographical references.
    ISBN 0-7852-8292-0 (pb)
    1. Adoption—United States.   2. Intercountry adoption—United States.
I. Duffy, Janice.   II. Title.
HV875.55.C73   1994
362.7'34—dc20   94-5607
                                                                                        CIP

Printed in the United States of America

1 2 3 4 5 6 7 - 00 99 98 97 96 95 94

To Katie, Andrea, and Courtney

The joy you have brought to our lives
made this book possible.

CONTENTS

Preface and Acknowledgments

We have spent many years working and talking with birthparents and adoptive couples. We are also adoptive parents. These experiences, as well as our own adoption experiences, have given us a personal understanding of the confusing and overwhelming process called adoption. Frequently we are approached by prospective adoptive parents who are looking for answers to their adoption questions. They are frustrated at the lack of accessible information in their local bookstores and libraries.

There is a need for basic, easily understandable adoption information. We talked with prospective and actual adoptive parents and then researched the answers to their most frequently asked questions. We interviewed adoption attorneys, doctors, social workers, and adoptive parents to provide the best possible up-to-date information. The result is this book.

How to Adopt a Child is set in a simple question-and-answer format. As you begin reading, the amount of information provided may seem a bit overwhelming. Do not be dismayed. We suggest you become familiar with the terms and definitions in the chapter titled "Some Adoption Terms," and then read the sections of the book that interest you. Each chapter ends with a summarized list of the questions and points previously covered to help you locate the questions and answers of interest to you.

Connie: My husband and I were unprepared for our adoption experience. We began discussing adoption as a possibility when it suddenly became a reality. A friend contacted us about an available child. We started searching for adoption information but were disappointed by what could be readily found. We did not have a clue as to how adoption works. We were unsure if private adoption was legal in our state. After much searching through the phone book we finally located an attorney who handled several adoption cases each year. He walked us through the process, carefully protecting our interest as well as the interest of the birth mother. Other adoptive parents we have known were not as lucky. They have chosen attorneys who knew little about the legalities of an adoption, thus leaving their adoptions on shaky legal ground. Most of the adoptive parents we have talked with said their own adoption experiences would have been smoother if they had been better informed about the adoption process.

Janice: My husband and I and our three children had been interested in adoption for many years. Following reports on TV in 1990 about the appalling conditions in Romanian orphanages, we decided to adopt one of these children. We searched but were able to find only a small amount of helpful information on foreign adoption. Traveling alone to Romania, I had little guidance. Our foreign adoption was a learn-as-you-go experience. A better understanding of the international-adoption process would have left me better prepared for the difficulties I encountered.

As adoptive parents we fully understand the joys and heartaches associated with adoption. This book is a result of our desire to reach out to people with adoption questions, whether they are prospective adoptive parents looking for a guide, grandparents seeking to understand adoption, birth parents who want to make informed adoption decisions, or anyone who wants simply to better understand the process of adoption.

We would like to thank all the people who helped us compile the answers to the questions presented in this book.

Our special thanks go to the following: Ronald G. Turner, Attorney at Law; Robert D. Tuke, Attorney at Law; and Mary B. Cooper. We appreciate all their legal assistance and guidance with adoption law. They are not responsible for the research and contents of this book.

Paul Douthitt, M.D., Robert A. Shearer, M.D., and John William O'Donnell, M.D., for their invaluable contributions and medical advice.

Sandy Ivey of Bethany Christian Services for her insights and input on agency adoption.

We are grateful to the many organizations that provided us with adoption information. We would especially like to express our appreciation to the National Adoption Clearinghouse for all their help and information.

We give special thanks to our wonderful editor at Thomas Nelson Publishers.

Our love and never-ending appreciation go to Connie's family (David, Courtney, Leon, Maxine, and Kristie) and to Janice's family (Roger, Aaron, Kristin, Adam, Andrea, and Katie) for all their patience, help, and understanding.

Chapter 1

THE BIG QUESTION

Are you considering adoption? If so, do you feel overwhelmed and discouraged by what you have heard about adoption today? You are not alone. More than a million couples each year consider adoption as a way to build a family. Of the thousands choosing to adopt, one out of thirty will succeed. Those that do not succeed often drop out prematurely due to frustration.

Do not let the statistics deter you. Adoption is possible today; whether you are married, single, or physically challenged, be assured that there is a child somewhere waiting for you. Preparation, determination, and perseverance are the key elements of all successful adoptions.

Who are the people considering adoption today? Each year one out of five couples is diagnosed as infertile. Although medical technology has made miraculous advancements toward the treatment of infertility, more and more couples choose adoption as a way to build a family.

Infertile couples are not the only ones looking into adoption. Today many families with children and an increasing number of single people are considering adoption. You may see yourself in one of the following profiles:

Beth and Thomas have tried unsuccessfully for eight years to conceive a child. In coming to terms with their infertility, they want to investigate the adoption process. Their first question is "How do we begin?"

Eric, age forty-five, and Tara, age forty-one, have been married eleven years. They have one teenage daughter, Lauren, from Tara's first marriage. For Tara, pregnancy is not an option. Their question is "Is adoption at our age a viable alternative for us?"

Rebecca and Richard have been married for fifteen years. They have three teenage children. The evening news reports of abandoned, starving children in Eastern Europe have touched their hearts. They would like to adopt one of these children. Their questions are "How risky is foreign adoption?" and "Is it expensive?"

Valerie is a single, thirty-three-year-old corporate executive. She feels she would be a good mother but does not want to go through a pregnancy. Valerie feels that adoption might be a good solution for her. She has heard that all healthy infants are placed with couples and that single people are considered only for children with special needs. Her question is "How can I adopt a healthy infant or young child?"

Stan and Charlotte are an African American couple with two children. They have heard through their church about the large numbers of black children who need adoptive homes, and they would like to provide a home for one of these children. Their question is "How can we afford the cost of adoption?"

The preceding case histories are based on real-life situations. Each prospective adoptive parent has his or her own needs and motivations, but all of them must decide if they want to adopt. Once that decision has been made, it's time to explore the various methods of adoption that are available.

There are four basic ways to adopt, and we will explore each one of them. They are as follows:

Agency adoption. Most people are familiar with this method. Licensed trained professionals mediate the adoption process between the adoptive parents and the birthmother from beginning to end.

Private adoption. This is the method in which adoptive parents normally locate a child without the assistance of an agency. An attorney then formalizes the process between the birthmother, the adoptive parents, and the court system.

State adoption. Social workers, under the direction of the Department of Child Welfare, mediate and oversee the adoption process.

International adoption. This term is used to indicate the adoption of a non-U.S. citizen. International adoption can be done privately or through an agency and must adhere to all federal and state regulations.

Adoption can be compared to going through a maze. Prospective adoptive parents often become misdirected and lost as they try to navigate the many twists and turns needed to complete an adoption.

Many times we have been approached by others seeking answers to their adoption questions. A common complaint among prospective adoptive parents is their frustration at the lack of adoption information, as well as the difficulty in understanding the information that is available. There are many good adoption resources out there, but they are difficult for the beginner to find. Our own adoption experiences and the information we gathered from other adoptive parents have provided us with a personal understanding of each type of adoption.

The first time you try anything complex, you need fundamental information. Unless you have spent years researching the subject of adoption, you will have many questions concerning the process.

We interviewed prospective adoptive parents and successful adoptive parents across the U.S. The following chapters contain the questions that prospective adoptive parents most frequently ask as they begin deciding if adoption is a viable option. Of course, one question often leads to many more, and we trust we will answer them or show you how to find the answers.

The answers proposed in this book were provided by attorneys, physicians, adoption agency spokespersons, state child and welfare social workers, the U.S. Immigration and Naturalization Service, and our own individual research. We have also included a resource chapter to give you a head start on your adoption investigation. Each resource will lead you to other excellent resources. Use this book as a guide to map your way through the maze called adoption.

Note: We have included legal information pertaining to specific adoption laws. However, because of the media attention that adoption has recently received, many states are currently reviewing and revising their adoption laws. It is imperative that you consult with a reputable attorney or adoption agency for specific laws adhered to by your state government.

Chapter 2

SOME ADOPTION TERMS

*T*his chapter covers frequently used adoption terms and their definitions. It is more than a simple glossary. The terms provided are intended to familiarize you with the adoption process and to help you begin thinking of some adoption questions that *you* want answered.

Abandonment   A situation in which one or both parents refuse physical, emotional, or financial support of their biological child.

Adoption   The legal process developed to allow biologically unrelated children and adults to form a family. The purpose of adoption is the permanent placement of children into loving and supportive homes that allow children to grow and reach their full potential.

Adoption benefits   A plan sponsored by a company or employer to provide financial assistance or monetary reimbursements toward adoption of a child by their employees.

Adoption counselor   A trained professional, often a social worker, who specializes in the adoption process. This person is knowledgeable in adoption law and understands the emotional needs of the birthparents as well as those of the adoptive parents. The counselor works on behalf of the birthparents, the adoptive parents, and the child, helping to meet the needs of everyone concerned.

Adoption disruption   The situation occurring when adoptive parents choose to revoke or discontinue an adoption.

Adoption finalization   Also known as the *adoption hearing*. The final step in the adoption process. An adoptive family appears in court before a judge, after submitting all the required adoption documents. The adoptive family swears before the judge that they have complied with all the necessary adoption requirements. The parents then promise to love and provide for the child to the best of their ability. A new birth certificate is issued with the adoptive parents listed as the child's parents and with the adopted child's name changed. The original birth certificate may be given to the adoptive parents. A copy of the original birth certificate is kept in the child's adoption records. The records are then sealed, and the adoption process is legally complete.

Adoption intermediary   Any nonagency third-party person (such as attorneys, doctors, counselors, clergy, or social workers) who works as a liaison between adoptive parents and birthparents. His or her goal is a satisfactory adoption agreement. It is important to note that some states consider nonagency third-party intervention illegal. Check with your state's regulations before you begin using an intermediary in a private adoption.

Adoption leave   Similar to a maternity leave, time away from work that a company provides for its employees to allow adoptive parents to bond with their new child. Adoption leave may be paid or unpaid time off from work; company policies vary. Currently a few companies offer adoption leave to fathers as well as to mothers.

Adoption petition   The legal document with which the prospective adoptive parents request permission from the court to adopt a specific child.

Adoption plan   The method of adoption chosen by the birthmother to best serve her needs and those of her baby. She may work with an agency, or she may locate and choose the adoptive parents herself. Each birthmother's adoption plan is individualized and includes the type and amount of contact she will have with her baby and the adoptive parents.

Adoption subsidies   Money provided to assist adoptive parents with the cost of an adoption. Federal and state governments provide money to assist with the adoption and care of a child with special needs. This plan was designed to remove any financial barriers that adoptive parents may face and allow them to adopt a difficult-to-place child.

Agency adoption   An adoption in which a privately funded, licensed adoption agency supervises and directs the adoption from start to finish. Fees are paid to the agency by the adoptive parents to cover the birthmother's expenses and the services rendered by the agency.

Birthfather   The biological father. If his identity is known, he must be included in the adoption procedure, and his parental rights must be surrendered before the adoption of the child can be completed. A man can prove paternity if he is named as the father on the child's birth certificate, or if genetic testing is positive. *Note:* In the event that a birthmother is married and she conceives a child during an extramarital affair, her husband is legally assumed by the court to be the "biological" father. The husband is then expected to surrender to the court his parental rights to the child being adopted.

Birthmother   The biological mother; the woman who gives birth to a child and then places the child for adoption.

Black-market adoption   An adoption in which large sums of money or items of value are traded for the placement of a child into an adoptive home. The money may be paid to the birthmother under the guise of "living expenses," or paid as a finder's fee to an intermediary. *Note:* This form of adoption constitutes the buying and selling of a child, and it is illegal.

CAP Book   A national photo-listing service that provides a state-by-state register of special-needs children available for adoption. The book provides pictures and descriptions of waiting children whom social workers have not been able to place through normal adoption channels.

Confidential records   The complete and original documents with all identifying information pertaining to the adoption. Once an adoption is finalized, all the records are sealed by the courts. These records may be opened only upon a judge's decree in any state.

Gray-market adoption   An adoption in which money is provided under the guise of questionable expenses for the birthmother. A court of law may rule gray-market adoption illegal.

Home study   The process in which a prospective adoptive parent or parents are evaluated to determine their suitability to parent a child. A completed home study is required in all states before an adoption can be legally finalized. A completed home study can be updated for subsequent adoptions with little difficulty. Most states consider a home study valid for one to five years.

Identified adoption   An adoption in which the adoptive parents and the birthparents locate each other. This is accomplished by word of mouth, personal recommendations, or advertisements in local newspapers. A licensed adoption agency is then chosen, usually by the adoptive parents, to act as an intermediary while providing the supervision and direction of the adoption process. The agency agrees to provide all of its available services to the birthparents and the adoptive parents. These services usually include counseling for the birthmother and the adoptive parents, support groups, and the preparation of the required home study. *Note:* This form of adoption may be used as an alternative in states in which nonlicensed, third-party, or private adoption is illegal.

I.N.S. The U.S. Department of Justice Immigration and Naturalization Service ("Immigrations"). Persons intending to adopt a child from a foreign country must file an I-600 or I-600A form with the I.N.S. in order for their adopted child to begin the process of obtaining a visa to enter the United States.

Inter-country contact This is the person adoptive parents locate to work on their behalf in an international adoption. The contact is usually a resident in the country where the adoption will occur, and is familiar with that country's culture. This person does much of the required "leg work" necessary for an international adoption (locating an available child, translating documents, hiring a lawyer, locating birthparents if required, locating a place for the adoptive couple to stay when they arrive in the contact's country). *Note:* Be alert. Some adoptive parents hiring the first friendly English-speaking person they met for their in-country contact have been unwittingly involved in black-market adoptions. These parents were forced to hand over large sums of money and still many were unable to complete an adoption.

Interlocutory decree This is a temporary court decree that sets the finalization of an adoption at a specific time in the future, usually six months to a year.

International adoption Also known as *intercountry adoption.* The legal adoption of a non-U.S. citizen under sixteen years old by an American parent or parents. International adoption can be carried out by a licensed agency or by an adoption intermediary. Adoptive parents must complete in behalf of the adopted child the naturalization process that all non-U.S. citizens must follow. Regulations governing international adoption can make the process lengthy and stress-ful, but it can be very successful. (*Note*: Adoption does not automatically give U.S. citizenship to a foreign-born child.)

Legal-risk adoption   An adoption in which a couple seeking to adopt agrees to be the foster parents for a child. This agreement is carried out with the understanding that the foster parents will adopt the child as quickly as legally feasible. Foster parents cannot assume any legal rights to the child until the legal adoption of the child is completed—a process that can take weeks, months, or years. The possibil-ity of birthparents choosing to keep their parental rights instead of relinquishing the child for adoption makes this a risky placement.

Licensed home study service agencies   Licensed compa-nies, located in several states across the U.S., that provide all the services associated with an adoption home study. Qualified social workers supervise and conduct home studies and postplacement visits. Postplacement visits are the visits a social worker makes after a child is placed with an adoptive family. These visits help a social worker observe how well the adoptive parents, as well as the child, are adjusting to family life. The social worker can provide home study updates and revisions on previous home studies for people adopting a second child. These agencies do not make adoption place-ments or work with birthparents.

Medical consent   A legal statement or form signed by the birthmother allowing an adoptive couple to make all medical decisions and to provide all medical care and treat-ments for the infant, beginning at birth.

The Mutual Consent and Voluntary Adoption Registries
The names of two separate agencies that work together to allow adult adoptees and biological parents to release identifying information. Adult adoptees and biological parents may arrange meetings together with the aid of counselors from these two agencies.

Naturalization   The process that allows a foreign-born child adopted by a U.S. citizen to become a U.S. citizen.

Nonidentifying information   Any information that does not reveal specific information about a person such as legal name, address, place of employment, or social security number. A person sharing nonidentifying information may say, "I live in a rural community in a two-story house with a big backyard and a dog. I am a preschool teacher who loves children. I come from a large, active, and athletic family, and I attended college." None of this information tells the person's identity, but it gives a general feel for the personality of the person speaking.

Open adoption   An adoption in which varying amounts of contact occur between the birthparents, the child being adopted, and the prospective adoptive parents. The amount of contact in an open adoption may range from the exchange of nonidentifying information to a complete exchange of identities. This can mean face-to-face meetings between birthparents and adoptive parents, and continued contact, including visits between the child, adoptive parents, and birthparents after the adoption finalization.

Open records   Adoption records that an adult adoptee is allowed access to. Currently only a few states allow an adult adoptee access to his or her sealed adoption records. A formal request to the courts to view the files is all that is required.

Prebirth consent   A legal document signed by a birthmother before her baby is born, indicating that she has surrendered her legal rights to her child to an adoptive parent or parents. This is allowed in a few states. *Note:* Not all states allow prebirth consents. Please check your local adoption laws.

Private adoption   Also known as *independent adoption*, this is an adoption arranged by the prospective adoptive parents and the birthmother with the assistance of someone other than an adoption agency. This assistance may come from an attorney or an adoption counselor, who works as an unbiased mediator.

Putative father   A man who was not married to the biological mother of his child at the conception or birth. He may attempt to establish his paternal rights through the courts or the Registry of Unwed Fathers.

The Registry of Unwed Fathers   A national service provided to assist an unwed father in establishing and protecting his individual rights to parent or support any biological child he may have fathered.

Revocation period   The designated period of time a state allows a birthmother to change her mind and stop the adoption process after she has surrendered her material rights to her child. The revocation period varies from state to state; it averages five to fifteen days but may be as short as two days or as long as six months.

Search and consent   The state's attempt, through the use of an adoption agency or other intermediary, to locate the biological parents on behalf of an adult adoptee. Once the agency has located the biological parents, a request for the release of identifying information is made. In the event that the biological parents refuse to allow the release of identifying information, the adult adoptee can file a petition with the court in which the adoption originated, and request that the confidential adoption records be opened and the information released. This process is legal in about one-fourth of the states in the U.S.

State adoption   Also known as *public agency adoption.* These adoptions are supervised and directed by each state's Child Welfare Protection Service through individual county offices. These state-funded agencies were developed to provide child protection services, foster care, special-needs programs, and adoption placements. These services are provided to the general public without regard to race, sex, or religious preference. These services are less expensive than private agency or independent adoption placements; in some cases the adoption may be done at no cost to the adoptive parents. The waiting period for healthy, white infants or young children can be lengthy, sometimes taking as long as ten years. Most children available for adoption through the state are older and/or are hard to place due to special needs. Each state adoption is conducted through the county that has jurisdiction over the child.

Surrender papers   Also known as *Consent to Adopt.* The legal document voluntarily signed by the birthparents, legal guardian, next of kin, or court-appointed friend. This document relinquishes all legal rights that a person has to a particular child. Once parental rights have been relinquished, the child may be adopted by another person or persons.

Visa　　An official permit providing legal entry into the country to which a person will be traveling. A visitor's visa is good for one to six months. An immigrant visa allows the adopted child to reside in the United States as a legal alien.

The following adoption terms are currently used to help remove the stigma and negative connotations formerly associated with adoption:

The terms *birthmother, birthfather,* and *birthparents* are used to replace the terms *"real" mother, "real" father,* and *"real" parents.* The term *"real" parents* in reference to the biological parents leads one to believe adoptive parents are not real or are inferior to the biological parents.

Adoptive children often experience identity crisis. To tell them they were put up for adoption or given away implies they were somehow less than acceptable. It is better to tell a child, "As a baby, you joined our family." It is better to say "Your birthparents terminated their parental rights" instead of saying "They gave you away" or "You were an unwanted child."

Never use the term *adoptive child* as a label. Some parents or grandparents have been heard introducing children by saying "This is my real son and this is my adopted son." This sends a message to your child and to others that he is different.

Chapter 3

AGENCY ADOPTION

When a prospective parent decides to investigate adoption, contacting an adoption agency can be a good place to begin gathering information. An agency may be local or national, state or privately funded. Licensed and trained professionals mediate the adoption process from start to finish in an agency adoption.

Locating and Choosing an Agency

We are considering adoption. Where can we get general information on adoption agencies?

Your state Child Welfare Office (the name of this agency can vary from state to state) can provide you with a free list of local licensed agencies, adoption support groups, and adoption conferences. You can find the number for the Child Welfare Office listed in the state government blue page section of your telephone directory. The white and yellow pages of the telephone directory contain numbers for any state adoption specialists, local agencies, or adoption information centers in your area.

How do we choose the right agency for us?

This is where your homework begins. You will want to determine whether or not the agencies you are considering are licensed. A license does not guarantee that an agency is ethical; however, it does indicate that the agency has the personnel and the ability to provide the services described on the license. Networking with those who have successfully adopted children is a good way to ensure your own success. Ask friends and relatives to recommend the names of other adoptive parents. Talk to these parents about how they viewed their agency.

Friends of ours say that agency adoption takes longer than private adoption. Is this true?

The process for an agency adoption requires the adoptive parents to complete an application for approval and a home study and then await the assignment of a child. This can take a few months to a few years. In a private adoption a couple actively seeks a birthmother, who may be recommended by a doctor, lawyer, or friend. This process can be quicker than an agency adoption.

Some agencies advertise that they are accredited. What does that mean?

The Council of Accreditation of Services for Families and Children, Inc. sets the standards of practice used to evaluate licensed agencies. Agencies pay an accreditation fee to be evaluated. Adoption agency accreditation is voluntary; it is not a mandatory requirement of all licensed adoption agencies. Accreditation can be valuable because it proves that an agency has exceeded the minimal state requirements for licensing. If an agency has not been evaluated by the Council of Accreditation, it does not necessarily indicate that the agency has questionable practices. The agency may be new or unable to afford the evaluation fees.

How can we contact the Council of Accreditation to receive a list of the agencies they have accredited?

Write to:
Council on Accreditation of Services for Families and Children, Inc.
520 8th Avenue, Suite 2202B
New York, NY 10018
(212) 714-9399

How can I find out if a particular agency is ethical in its practices?

You may want to contact your state attorney general's office and the local Office of Consumer Affairs or the Better Business Bureau. You will be able to find out if any formal complaints have been lodged against a specific adoption agency.

How can we determine if an agency shares our views on adoption?

Review the mission statement of all the agencies you consider. You may also want to note the policies and practices of any organization of which the agency is a member. It is important to choose an agency that you feel comfortable with from the beginning. Contact the agency and ask them to send you their mission statement.

What is a mission statement?

A mission statement is the written goals, business beliefs, and practices of an agency. It may or may not be religious in nature.

Several agencies appeal to us. Where do we go from here?

Contact all the agencies that interest you and request a set of their guidelines. Adoption agencies have varied requirements that prospective adoptive parents should consider. *Beware:* Typically, application fees are nonrefundable, so be sure to understand an agency's terms and conditions of adoption before sending an application fee.

Will an agency meet with me before I decide to definitely work with them?

Many agencies schedule orientation meetings for prospective adoptive parents. These sessions allow you to meet adoption social workers and become informed about the agencies' policies and practices. You are on a fact-finding mission, so do not limit yourself to just one agency. Attend as many orientation seminars as possible, and list your questions before you attend the meeting. Host counselors are generally willing to schedule an appointment with you to address any additional concerns. Take notes at each meeting you attend, and list your likes and dislikes about the agency. Then compare the pros and cons of all the agencies.

What are some of the specific things discussed in an orientation meeting?

The agency's representatives will address the availability of infants and the amount of time it will take to place an infant in your home. They will also discuss the types of children available. You should receive information on the agency's adoption process, fees, and general requirements. The agency will tell you exactly what they are looking for in prospective parents. This is a good opportunity to ask questions.

Cost

We are worried that we will not be able to afford to adopt. How much will an agency adoption cost?
The cost for adopting can range from a low of $5,000 to a high of $25,000. Many agencies determine the cost of adoption by using a sliding scale based on the couple's combined gross annual income. The cost may be less if you are considering a special needs child.

Adoption Agency Services

Do adoption agencies provide any services besides placing children?
Yes. Many agencies today provide pregnancy counseling, pregnancy crisis hotlines, and infant foster care while birthmothers decide whether to parent or to place their children for adoption. In addition, some agencies provide foster care for older children who have been neglected or abused. Some agencies even provide residential treatment for birthmothers, family counseling, child care services, refugee services, and outreach to families in crisis.

Religious Requirements

Do all agencies require adoptive parents to belong to a church or synagogue?
No. A number of agencies have no religious requirements. An agency requiring a specific religious affiliation usually

requests references from the prospective adoptive parents' church or synagogue.

Several agencies use the names of religious organizations in their title. Do these agencies service only persons affiliated with that specific religion?
In your adoption search you may come across agencies such as Jewish Family Services, Catholic Charities, Christian Counseling Services, and Lutheran Social Services. Do not disqualify an agency solely because of its name. An agency may have been originally founded or financially supported by a particular church or organization. Today, some agencies have expanded their services to place children with families who are not affiliated with a specific religious organization or church. Catholic Charities generally requires one of the applicants to be a practicing member of a Catholic church. Some Jewish Family Services agencies require applicants to be of the Jewish faith, while others have no requirements for religion. Bethany Christian Services requires applicants to be active members of an evangelical church, and the applicants must sign a statement of faith. A phone call to these agencies can quickly answer this question.

What is a statement of faith?
A statement of faith is a form written and signed by applicants to adoption agencies affiliated with a religious organization which states the applicant's religious beliefs.

Working with an Agency

To increase our chances for a successful adoption, should we work with more than one agency at a time?
At the beginning of your adoption process, put your name on

as many agency waiting lists as possible. Your name can remain on the waiting list an average of six months to a year before you are contacted by the agency to be placed on their prospective adoptive parent list. When an agency calls to tell you that they are ready to begin your home study, you will need to work exclusively with that agency.

What happens if I get pregnant while working with an agency? Can we remain on the adoption list if we want to?
If you become pregnant during the adoption process, the agency will put your file on hold until after the delivery. If you miscarry or the baby is stillborn, you will not have lost your place on the agency's list. After you have had a successful delivery, the agency will make your file inactive.

If we are working with an agency and the baby they have chosen for us is born with severe medical problems, will we be responsible for the medical bills?
The agency will inform you if the baby is having medical problems. It will be your choice whether to accept the baby and the medical conditions or to wait for another child. While the baby is still in the hospital with the birthmother, the baby is covered under the birthmother's insurance or her Medicaid or Medicare. If the baby has to have an extended hospital stay, the agency will sign up the baby for its own Medicaid, as the baby is not yet legally yours but is technically in the foster care system. If extensive medical treatment is required, groups such as the Shriners can be called upon to help for certain medical conditions. Medicaid can continue two or three weeks and be renewed until the child has been placed in your home.

Considering Special Needs

If we meet with the birthmother through our agency and the baby is born with a serious medical condition we don't feel we can handle, are we obligated to adopt that child? Can we wait for another baby?

When you begin the adoption process, you will be asked to fill out a medical condition sheet so that the agency will know in advance what you feel you can and cannot handle. They will also extensively interview you to help you explore your true feeling about various medical conditions. Consider this sheet very carefully. (You may be willing, for example, to accept a child with a club foot but not with cerebral palsy.) You will not be obligated to take a child you feel you cannot handle. The agency wants to do what is best for you and what is best for the baby. If you are willing to consider a child with a medical problem, you should ask to be given a complete medical summary. Request an independent medical evaluation of the child by a pediatrician of your choice. This will prevent any misleading information or misunderstandings from occurring between you and the agency. Any infant placed for adoption should receive a preadoptive physical, and the report should be given to the adoptive parents.

What will we be asked to consider on the medical condition sheet?

- Low birth weight
- Premature birth
- Heart defects
- Hepatitis B carrier
- Blood disorders
- Hermaphroditism (a rare condition in which both

ovarian and testicular tissues are present within the
same infant, thus requiring corrective surgery)
- A missing limb due to an accident
- A condition that confines the child to a wheelchair
- Spina bifida (a congenital malformation of the spine
  which usually results in multiple chronic disabilities
  for the child)
- Cerebral palsy
- A postpolio condition
- Orthopedic problems
- Rickets
- A congenital hip defect
- Malformations of the body
- Vision problems
- Hearing problems
- Diabetes
- Epilepsy
- Cleft lip
- Severe malnutrition
- Kidney malfunction
- Burns requiring plastic surgery
- Developmental delays
- Emotional problems

Consider the medical conditions very carefully. You will be
asked to consider each condition by the degree of severity you
are willing to accept. You will also be asked to simply mark yes,
no, or maybe to each condition. Children with these types of
problems need families who will nurture and love them. Deciding
to accept a child with one of the problems in the preceding list
can shorten your waiting time for a child. *Note:* See chapter
titled "Medical Conditions" for an overview of a few of the
medical conditions you will be asked to consider.

What does an agency consider a normal, healthy infant?
Years ago a normal, healthy infant was a child of your race with good health and who matched your physical appearance. Today a normal, healthy child is still a child in good health and of your race but can include children of mixed heritage. *Note:* In some areas of the country a healthy black or half-black infant or child is considered a special-needs placement.

When we received paperwork from one agency we contacted, they asked us if we would consider a special-needs child. What does an agency consider to be a special-needs child?
Special-needs children include children with handicaps and medical conditions but can also mean hard-to-place children. Hard-to-place children are biracial or black children, sibling groups, and older children. An Asian or half-Asian child is not considered a special-needs placement. In some parts of the country a Hispanic child may or may not be considered a special-needs placement, depending on the agency. See the chapter titled "State and Special-Needs Adoption" for more information.

Can a physically disabled person adopt a child?
Every agency has its own requirements for adoption. Generally, people with disabilities can adopt. The disability will be assessed, and if it doesn't stand in the way of the person's parenting skills, the person will be approved as an adoptive parent.

Birthmothers

We are nearing completion on an adoption through an agency. We have now heard of a birthmother who wants

to place her child for adoption independently. Can we adopt both children at the same time?

Yes. The agency will not prevent you from adopting privately. You cannot, however, adopt from two agencies simultaneously.

If a child is scheduled for placement in our home and the birthmother changes her mind, will we be considered for the next available infant, or will our money be refunded?

Many agencies today let the birthmother choose the adoptive parents. If a birthmother changes her mind, the agency places your file back into the pool from which other birthmothers can choose. If your agency operates on the basis of a list, you will be considered for the next available child. Or you can choose to have your money refunded.

How do agencies locate the birthmothers who want to place their babies for adoption?

Agencies locate the birthmothers through crisis pregnancy centers, word of mouth, flyers, school counselors, clergy, and so on. *Note:* Only 1.5 out of every ten pregnant girls make adoption plans.

The agency that we want to work with lets the birthmother choose the couple who will adopt her baby. What if a birthmother doesn't choose us?

If for some reason a birthmother doesn't choose you, the agency will work to match you with a compatible birthmother. Some birthmothers don't want to know anything about the adoptive family. The agency will decide on a family according to the birthmother's needs and wishes.

**Will the birthmother ever be asked to base her decision
on a picture of us? What if she doesn't like our looks?**
The birthmother is given profiles of all of the prospective
adoptive parents, and she chooses a family based on those
profiles. Pictures may or may not be used in the initial
process. The birthmother is asked not to make a decision
based on a photograph of the prospective adoptive parents.

**We know of a girl who wants to put her baby up for
adoption. Will an agency help us adopt that baby?**
Using an agency for adopting a baby that you yourself have
located is called a designated placement. Most agencies will
help you complete such an adoption. The birthmother has
the final say.

**Once the child has been placed in our home, how long
does the birthmother have to change her mind?**
The time will vary from state to state. From the date that a
birthmother relinquishes her child in court, she has five to
fifteen days in most states to change her mind about the
adoption. The days are *not* counted from the birth of the
baby or from the day that the child is placed in the adoptive
home.

Open Adoption

We hear the term "open adoption" a lot. What does it mean?
Open adoption refers to the amount of information exchanged
between the adoptive parents and the birthparents. The
birthmother chooses the degree of openness in the relationship. It can range from a one-time letter exchange to a
face-to-face meeting between the two parties through the

agency to an ongoing relationship between the adoptive family and the birthmother.

Do we have to agree to open adoption in order to adopt today?

No, but it is important to carefully consider the amount of information you feel comfortable exchanging. The more receptive you are to information exchange, the more open your options will be. If you want no contact with the birthmother, the agency will still work with you since there are birthmothers who want no contact with the adopting family. Some agencies will provide the birthmother with a monthly report and pictures of the baby during the first year.

What are the benefits of an open adoption?

There are a number of benefits for all parties involved in an open adoption. In an open adoption a birthmother is given the opportunity to meet the people who will become the parents of her baby. Many birthmothers feel more secure with their adoption decisions after they have met or spoken to the adoptive parents. The meeting helps a birthmother feel that her child is going to a loving home, and dispels the feeling that she is giving her baby to strangers. A great number of adoptive parents who favor open adoptions feel that a meeting with the birthmother decreases their own fears and anxieties about the adoption process. Yet the greatest benefit is to the child being adopted. It is important to plan ahead for the time when your adopted child may have serious questions about his or her birth family. Medical history can prove invaluable. Your child may want to know the birthfather's occupation, what color eyes the birthmother has, whether she liked to read, or whether she was athletic. The answers to these questions allow a child to look to both the adoptive family and the birth family to help piece together his or her identity.

We are not comfortable with the idea of an open adoption. What should we do?

Nowhere is it stated that open adoptions are mandatory. You must decide what is and what is not acceptable to you before you begin the adoption process. Do not feel guilty about your decisions if they are for the child's benefit as well as your own. If you are not comfortable with a meeting or an exchange of letters with a birthmother, we encourage you to at least ask her to fill out a medical history form for herself and her immediate family. If at all possible, you should try to obtain a medical history from the birthfather as well as medical information concerning his immediate family. This information can prepare you for any possible health risks your child may face. If you live in a relatively small town and adopt a child from your area, it can be important to know whether your adoptive child has any brothers or sisters that he or she may unknowingly date in later years.

Interstate Adoption

We were told by a family friend about a great adoption agency in another state. Does it cost more to adopt out of state?

Yes. Living and travel expenses can add considerably to the cost of out-of-state adoption.

Matching Adoptive Parents with a Child

How will an agency choose a baby for us?

Many agencies today allow the birthmother to choose the

adoptive family. She is given profiles of prospective adoptive parents who closely match the type of family she wants for her child. She will select an adoptive family from these profiles. A few adoption agencies will match the birthmother with the adoptive parents themselves.

What is a profile?
A profile is a light resume of the prospective adoptive parents. This short biography helps the birthmother choose her baby's adoptive family.

What type of information will we be asked to give on our profile? Will we be asked to give any identifying information?
You will be asked to provide general, nonidentifying information on your profile. The following includes the specific information you may be asked to provide:

- General family information, including the ages of the husband, wife, and children; date of marriage; date of the adoption application; a description of your home, community, and church
- Physical characteristics—height, build, complexion, eye color, hair color, and nationality
- Education—degree completed and major
- Employment, including total income
- Plans for future employment
- Personality characteristics
- Hobbies and interests
- Pets
- Family characteristics and background, including relatives
- Any other information you feel is important for the birthmother to know
- The adoption agency staff may include in the profile a list of their recommendations and a summary

We heard that a baby may come to us from temporary foster care. What does that mean?

An agency will place an infant in foster care when they are unable to place the baby directly in the adoptive home. Foster homes are licensed by the agency or state to give temporary care to the child until the child goes home with the adoptive family. The agency places the baby in foster care if they feel that the birthmother is wavering in her adoption decision. This is one advantage of working with an agency. The foster-care system protects the adoptive family emotionally in case the birthmother changes her mind and decides to keep her child.

We have two children and would like to adopt. Do agencies have a family size limit?

Many agencies prefer working with childless couples or couples with no more than one child. Others have no limits on family size. Even agencies preferring to work with childless couples will make an exception for the adoption of special-needs children.

My husband and I are taller than average and are of Italian heritage. Will an agency give us a baby that looks like us?

While physical appearance is usually the last thing that an agency considers in the placement of a child, there are some exceptions. The general height of the family may be a consideration. An adoptive couple whose family height averages five feet four inches will not usually be matched to a child whose birth-family height averages six feet two inches. A birthmother will choose an adoptive family based on the prospective parents' profile, not based on a picture. Through questions asked during the initial interviews, your social worker will attempt to determine if you have come to terms with your infertility. You will be advised to bury the image of the child you have carried in your heart for so many years and be prepared to accept and love the child who will come into your home, regardless of that child's looks or coloring. However, some agencies will allow African American families to inquire about the skin coloring of a child prior to placement of the child in their home.

Our adoption agency asked us to consider a legal risk placement. What does this mean?
A legal risk placement occurs when the adoptive parents agree to take the child they intend to adopt into their home before all the legal aspects of the surrender of parental rights have been met. For example, the adoptive parents may take a child home before the birthmother or birthfather has signed the Consent to Adopt (surrender of their rights), or perhaps the surrender has been signed but the revocation period has not yet passed. Taking the child home at these times is a risk because the prospective adoptive home is legally considered a temporary foster home and the adoptive parents have no legal claims to the child they wish to adopt.

If we adopt a baby privately and take the child home with us before the waiting period (revocation) is over, is this a legal risk placement?
Yes, because the birthmother or birthfather can still legally change his or her mind and stop the adoption process. The story of baby Jessica was based on this situation. The adoptive parents had the baby at home, and the birthmother changed her mind during the legally allotted time. The child remained in the prospective adoptive home during a legal suit but eventually was returned to the birthmother.

We feel we can handle a legal risk placement. Are there any special considerations we should think about?

Many adoptive parents accept legal risk placements without difficulty. If you currently have a young child living in your home, consider the possible effects of a legal risk placement to that child. Bringing an infant into your home only to return him to the birthparents may adversely affect your child. Will she think the baby was returned because he was the "wrong" one? Will your child become concerned she will be taken from her home if you decide she is the "wrong kid"? The age and understanding of your child will help you determine how to handle your individual situation.

The Home Study

What is a home study, and who needs one?

Today, people who are seeking to adopt, whether they are single or married, must have an adoption home study. The home study provides prospective adoptive parents with the opportunity to document who they are. A social worker interviews the applicants and collects in-depth information about them. During this process the applicants are asked to answer questions and to provide documents such as their marriage license, any divorce decrees, their birth certificates, and their medical and financial statements. These documents give the courts and the agency an accurate account of the applicants and their home life. During the home-study process, the prospective adoptive parents meet with their social workers several times in their home as well as in the social worker's office. The home study helps determine their suitability as adoptive parents.

Who is in charge of a home study?

The agency or state department of social services has a social worker assigned as a caseworker to the prospective adoptive parents. It is this social worker's job to guide prospective adoptive parents through the home-study process, answer questions, and file the compiled data into a report that will be presented to the court at the adoption finalization.

How long will a home study take?

The length of a home study varies from agency to agency. An average of two to three months is typical, but it can take from six months to one year for a social worker to complete your home study.

We are anxious to begin the actual adoption. How can we speed up the process of completing our home study?

Cooperate with your caseworker. Fill out all of the paperwork promptly and quickly. Don't put off scheduling your medical appointments, and do begin to gather all the documents and certified copies immediately.

How long will our home study be valid?

A home study is usually valid for one year, with the exception of sudden life changes such as divorce, death, or unemployment. Should it take more than one year to adopt from the completion of your home study, the home study can easily be updated by your social worker.

How much will the home study cost?

A public agency such as the department of social services in your state may charge only a modest fee to complete a home study. Adoption agencies charge five hundred to two thousand dollars for a completed home study, with the average cost today being twelve hundred dollars. The home study fee can be decreased or waived when you are adopting a special-needs child.

We were foster parents three years ago. Can we use our foster care home study in place of our adoption home study?
Ask your social worker if your home study can be updated. If no significant changes have taken place in your life, the foster care home study may be used, and may save you part of the cost of an adoption home study.

Can the home-study requirement ever be waived?
No. All states today require a home study in every situation. For those who adopt privately, a certified social worker in private practice may be hired to conduct the home study. The adoptive parents may also choose to contact an adoption agency to complete the home study.

What documents will we need for our home study?
- Certified copies of birth certificates for yourself, your spouse, and any children
- A certified copy of your marriage license
- Certified copies of divorce decrees, if applicable
- Certified copies of the finalization or adoption decree from any previously adopted children
- Criminal record clearances or a notarized statement from the police stating that there have been no felony convictions against you
- Financial statements, which may include tax returns, W-2 forms, paycheck stubs, and a notarized statement from your bank on you as a customer
- A life history you've written about yourself—called the autobiography

- Social Security numbers
- A statement of health, provided by your physician and following a physical exam, lab-test results, and possibly a letter of infertility
- Written references

In addition, if either the husband or the wife was previously widowed, copies of the death certificate and previous marriage certificate may also be requested. Also, note that some religious-affiliated agencies require a statement of faith.

Our social worker told us to be thorough and accurate when filling out our autobiographies. What kinds of questions can we expect?
You can expect questions in each of the following categories:

- **Your background:** Your childhood, family life, and the kinds of relationships you had with your parents, siblings, and extended family
- **Education:** Your level of education and any plans to continue your education. Also, your views on the child's education
- **Your employment record:** Your employment history. You may be asked to provide a letter from your employer, stating your job function and salary
- **Your marriage:** How long you and your spouse dated, the length of your marriage, how you make decisions and solve conflicts, how you communicate your feelings, and any other previous marriages and how long they lasted
- **Your hobbies and interests:** How you spend your leisure time, and what clubs, organizations, and community activities you participate in

- **Your community and neighborhood:** The location, surroundings, and community resources available that will benefit your child, such as schools, parks, hospitals, and your plans for child care if needed
- **Your religion:** Your religious beliefs and the importance they play in your life, your level of religious practice, and what type of religious upbringing you intend to provide for your child, if any
- **Adoption-related issues:** Why you want to adopt; what kind of child you feel you can best parent; how you will tell your child about his or her adoption; how you will handle adoption-related questions from family members, friends, and strangers; and how you feel about raising a child not related to you
- **Your experiences with children:** Any work with children through your community, your church, baby-sitting, coaching, and so on. You may be asked "What if . . . ?" or "How would you handle this?" questions in regard to discipline and your views on parenting

My husband is under a doctor's care for hypertension. Will this disqualify us as adoptive parents?
Generally, a person who is under a physician's care and who has a health problem controlled by diet or medication will not be disqualified on the basis of that medical condition. A serious medical condition that affects a person's life expectancy may prevent approval. A person who is HIV-positive can be approved as an adoptive parent of an HIV-positive or AIDS-infected child in some cases.

Our friends who have adopted a child have told us that we will be required to provide the agency with a health

statement during the home-study process. What is a health statement?

A health statement is simply a letter or form completed by your physician, stating that you are healthy, that you are emotionally and physically able to raise a child, and that you have a normal life expectancy. You may be asked if you smoke. Agencies will require you to have a thorough medical exam, including a tuberculosis test. Some states and many agencies require a prospective adoptive parent to be tested for AIDS prior to approval for adoption.

Our home-study packet includes forms for fingerprints. What do we do with these forms?

Many states require a criminal-record check. To do this, take the fingerprint forms to your local police station. A police official will fingerprint you free of charge and will run your name through the police computers to see if you have any prior child-abuse or criminal records on file. This is done for the protection of the child. To obtain police clearance without being fingerprinted, in some instances you can send a notarized form with your name, date of birth, and Social Security number to the child welfare office or to a local police agency. Your social worker will tell you what is required for your state. *Note:* Any misdemeanor that you committed during your teens or early twenties will usually not be held against you. If you have any felony convictions for illegal drug use, you will be questioned extensively and asked to prove and substantiate your life-style change. Child abuse convictions will not be tolerated.

My husband and I have a moderate income. Do we have to earn a certain amount of money to adopt?

Wealth is not a requirement for adoption. The agency and

courts simply want to know if you can financially provide for the child you are adopting.

How will we be asked to verify our income?

Verifying your income is similar to applying for a credit card. You will be asked to provide a record of your income through an employment letter, tax records, W-2 forms, or paycheck stubs. You will need a letter from your bank stating your financial history and listing your assets and debts such as savings accounts, mortgages, insurance policies, car payments, and charge accounts.

What importance does religion have on the outcome of a home study?

When working with an agency that is associated with a religious group, your religious beliefs will be considered very important. The social worker may request a letter of recommendation from your pastor, priest, or rabbi. Nonreligious agencies may simply request a statement of your religious beliefs, if any, for their records.

Our social worker said we need four letters of reference. Whom do we ask for these letters?

Anyone who has known you very well over a number of years can be a good reference. You may ask close friends, your employer, former teachers, coworkers, neighbors, family friends, or clergy. You will want to choose people who know you best and who can comment favorably on your life-style. Include any friends who have seen how you interact with children.

If we get a bad reference, will we be denied approval for adoption?

One negative reference will usually not be enough to deny

adoption approval. The social worker may call the person who gave the reference in order to further discuss that person's negative comments. If you receive several negative references, the social worker will investigate you much more closely.

We have heard that a social worker will visit our home. What will he or she be looking for?
The social worker will be looking closely at the environment in which the adopted child will be living. Some questions that the social worker will need to answer include the following:

- Is the environment safe? Are you aware of how to make your home childproof?
- Do you have smoke alarms in the proper places? Do you have an evacuation plan in case of fire?
- Will your house provide a clean, healthy environment for the child?
- How many rooms are in the house? Where will your child sleep?
- Where will the child play? The social worker may also check your backyard and basement.

We have a five-year-old biological son. Will he be included in the home study?
Any child, adopted or biological, who is living in the home will be included in your home study. Your child will be required to have a physical exam and will be interviewed to assess his adjustment to a new family member. The social worker will need a certified copy of your child's birth certificate (and adoption records if applicable). A child's input is seen as important in the overall assessment of the family's readiness and ability to provide a home for an additional child.

How can we improve and personalize our home study?
Write your autobiography to express your personality, and be sure to list all the experiences you have had with children. Include photos of your family, home, neighborhood, pets, close friends, relatives, and grandparents. Ask the social worker to keep the photos with your file.

Bringing the Baby Home

From the time the agency contacts us to say they have a baby for us, how soon will we be able to bring the baby home?
The time varies. In a private adoption or legal-risk placement the newborn can be discharged from the hospital nursery straight to the adoptive home. Many agencies, private and state, will place the newborn into foster care (interim care) until the revocation period of the adoption has passed. This may be as little as two weeks or as long as six months.

How long does it usually take to finalize an adoption?
Once a child is placed in an adoptive home, the time required by the courts before finalization occurs varies from state to state. Some states require as little as one week, while others require one year from the date of placement.

A Summary of the Steps Required for an Agency Adoption

1. Locate various adoption agencies that interest you.
2. Ask for the complete list of adoption requirements and guidelines from each of those agencies.
3. Make a list of the questions you need to have answered by the adoption agencies.

4. Arrange a meeting with the persons from the two agencies you would most like to work with.
5. Choose an adoption agency and complete an adoption application. A nonrefundable application fee may be required at this time.
6. Discuss with your social worker the kind of child you would like to adopt—for example, a newborn, a sibling group, a biracial child, a healthy child of your race, or a disabled child.
7. Begin your adoption home study with your social worker. Gather the necessary documents, such as marriage certificates, birth certificates, financial statements, and personal references. Also, be sure that each member of your household is given (or has been recently given) a complete medical examination.
8. Pay the required fees in a timely manner to the agency. If you are having financial difficulties, make alternative arrangements with your agency.
9. Following contact by the agency, accept the assignment of a child.
10. Go to the surrender hearing where the birthparents relinquish parental rights and you accept legal guardianship of the child.
11. Wait for the duration of the revocation period. The infant may go into foster care during this time or may be placed directly into the adoptive home during this period.
12. File the Petition to Adopt forms with the necessary courts. The agency, your lawyer, or you, yourself, can file.
13. Legally finalize your adoption with the appropriate courts in a timely manner. In addition to the agency personnel, an adoption attorney may be needed to complete this step. Finalization occurs three months to one year following placement, depending on individual state laws.

Chapter 4

PRIVATE ADOPTION

*T*he majority of adoptions today are completed privately. Many people like the control and freedom that private adoption affords. In private adoption the prospective adoptive parents and the birthmother arrange the adoption together or through an intermediary. Done properly and with the help of a knowledgeable adoption attorney, a private adoption may be faster and more cost-effective than an agency adoption. On the downside, private adoption can be emotionally risky. This chapter will help you decide if private adoption is for you.

The Private Adoption Choice

What is independent or private adoption?

Independent or *private adoption* means the placement of a child in an adoptive home without the help of an agency. In private adoption a couple may actively seek a birthmother through an intermediary or through advertising. The adoptive family will complete the adoption with the help of an attorney.

What is the difference between an agency adoption and a private adoption?
In an agency adoption a couple files an application and waits for approval by the agency, who is then responsible for placing an infant with the adoptive family. In a private adoption a couple actively tries to locate a child to adopt. The responsibility of completing the adoption lies with the adoptive family.

What are some of the advantages of private adoption?

- A private adoption may be quicker.
- A private adoption may be less expensive.
- A private adoption lends itself more readily to being "open." The birthparents and adoptive parents can choose to become acquainted and to continue personal contact after the adoption.
- Many times in private adoptions the birthmother lets the adoptive parents be present in the delivery room with her.

What are some of the disadvantages of private adoption?
When adopting privately, you will be able to bring the baby directly home from the hospital. While this may be seen as an advantage by many, having the baby in your home during the time that the birthmother is allowed to change her mind (the revocation period) can lead to heartbreak. You can choose someone to keep the baby for you during this time,

but most adoptive parents do not choose this alternative. Some prospective adoptive parents choose agency adoption over private adoption because they find comfort in working with an established agency during the adoption process. If problems arise, the agency may be better equipped in assisting the adoptive parents through the emotional stress.

The Choice of an Attorney

My brother-in-law studied law for one year. He would like to help us complete our adoption to save money. Do we have to use an attorney to complete our adoption?
It is advisable to use an attorney in an independent adoption. Laws vary from state to state, and it is important to work with an attorney who is knowledgeable in the field of adoption. If you begin working with a reputable attorney early in the process, you will be able to alleviate some of the stress and unnecessary problems you may encounter along the way. Your attorney will be able to give you suggestions and to solve problems to help guide you through the adoption process.

How do we choose an attorney that is right for us?
Begin by interviewing several attorneys in your area over the phone. You can get names of adoption attorneys by calling the local bar association for referrals. Some attorneys advertise in the yellow pages of the phone book that they handle adoption cases. Adoptive parent support groups in your area can be a valuable resource for recommending reputable attorneys.

What should we ask the attorneys we interview?
Diane Michelsen, J.D., M.S.W., in her article for *Ours* (January/February 1993) lists seven topics you should address

when choosing an attorney. Some of the questions you will need to ask the attorneys you interview are as follows:

1. **Philosophy:** What is the attorney's general philosophy about adoption? How does the attorney view open and closed adoptions? Will the attorney be willing to adjust to your needs and desires? What does the attorney consider his or her role to be in the adoption process?

2. **Expertise:** Is the attorney experienced, knowledgeable, and competent? How many adoptions does the attorney do each year? Ask for references.

3. **Billing:** What is the cost of an average adoption? How does the attorney bill—by set fees or by the hour?

4. **Accessibility:** Will the attorney return phone calls, and when? Will the attorney's office staff keep you up to date on the progress of your adoption? Will they send you copies of all important documents? Will the attorney adjust to your wishes? Will the attorney accept collect phone calls from the birthmother? Is the attorney available for emergencies after hours and on the weekends? If your attorney cannot be reached, will another knowledgeable attorney be available to answer your questions?

5. **Counseling:** Does the attorney believe that counseling is helpful for the birthmother? Will the attorney assist in locating a counselor for the birthmother if necessary?

6. **Assistance:** Will the attorney actively assist you in locating a birthmother as well as in handling the legal work for the adoption? How successful has the attorney been in the past in locating a birthmother?

7. **Personalities:** How do you feel about the attorney and the attorney's office staff? Do they put you at ease? Will they be gracious and kind to the birthmother?

We have decided to pursue private adoption. At what point in the process should we locate an attorney?

The process of finding a good adoption attorney may take some time. Begin interviewing attorneys at the very beginning of your adoption process to avoid the stress and panic of searching through the phone book after you have located a birthmother.

The attorney-client relationship can continue for many months before and even following the adoption. You should feel comfortable asking questions, and you should feel that the attorney cares and will work diligently for you throughout the adoption process. (Many attorneys will meet with you in person only once, as most of the work will be handled in writing and over the phone.)

The Home Study

Is a private adoption home study different from an agency home study?

No. Required home studies are the same whether you are adopting privately or through an agency. Home-study requirements can vary from agency to agency and from state to state. Basically, in conducting a home study, all social workers require you to participate in interviews, fill out paperwork, obtain medical exams, and provide a written account of your life. *Note:* For more in-depth information, read the section "The Home Study" in the chapter titled "Agency Adoption."

Birthmothers

Why do birthmothers choose private adoption?

There are various reasons why a birthmother may choose independent adoption. Sometimes she wants more control over the adoption. Her financial needs may come into play. She may feel uncomfortable or too embarrassed to talk with an agency counselor.

We are considering private adoption, but we don't feel comfortable with open adoption. Does private adoption mean we will have to meet with the birthparents?
A successful private adoption does not have to have an "open" arrangement. You will need to consider how much contact and exchange of information you are willing to have before you begin interviewing birthmothers. It is important to work with a reputable attorney from the beginning, so that he or she can assist you in your contact with the birthmother. Some birthmothers want to meet the adoptive parents; others want to exchange first names only. Your attorney will be very helpful with this matter. Remember that in private adoption the birthmother is usually in control. She may change her mind on how much contact she wants with you as the adoption proceeds. Understanding this fact from the beginning will help prevent frustration and confusion later.

When we locate a birthmother who is willing to work with us, what things should we consider? What questions should we ask the birthmother?
Ask her for the following information:

- A brief history of her background, including her age, whether she has other children, and who she lives with
- What she is looking for in an adoptive family
- A description of her pregnancy. How far into her pregnancy is she? Is she under a physician's care, and if so, at what point in her pregnancy did she begin prenatal care?

- Whether she is on Medicare or Medicaid. If not, does she have insurance?
- Whether she would be willing to talk with your attorney

We've been told by our attorney that the birthmother wants a face-to-face meeting. We're afraid we'll say something wrong and she'll change her mind. Are there any guidelines we need to follow?

Take a deep breath and relax. The birthmother did not request the meeting to hunt for flaws in you as a person. This is a woman who needs reassurance. The burden of placing a child for adoption is not a small one. She may simply want to know you better. Think of this meeting as an opportunity to exchange histories, and not as a test that you must pass or fail. Exchange only the information you feel comfortable offering. Be direct, honest, and sincere. You may want to make a list of questions to ask her. Give her the option of expressing her opinions and views concerning the adoption. Try to remember that everyone involved is working toward the same goal—placing a child in a loving home.

Personal Considerations

My wife and I have been turned down by an adoption agency because I am forty-five years old and she has been married before. Are there any restrictions such as age and marital status when adopting privately?

Age and marital status are not factors when adopting privately. Many couples find that they can successfully adopt privately after being turned down by an adoption agency.

Cost

How much should we expect a private adoption to cost?
Private adoption costs can range anywhere from five thousand to forty thousand dollars. Your costs may run lower if your birthmother lives at home and has good health insurance or if she is on Medicaid. Attorney fees can make a big difference in the total adoption cost, depending on whether they are based on an hourly rate or on a flat fee. A good private adoption attorney will complete the work in less time than someone who is unfamiliar with the field. Adoption costs can go much higher than you expected if the birthmother requires a cesarean section or if the baby is hospitalized for an extended period. Some doctors and hospitals will not accept Medicare or Medicaid payments; in these situations the adoptive parents are responsible for all medical costs associated with the birth of the baby.

We have limited finances. What are some things we can do to cut our adoption costs?

- Adopt in your own state. This will cut traveling costs and additional attorney fees that may be required in another state.
- Work with a birthmother who has insurance and who will use her insurance for the birth of the baby.
- If the birthmother does not have medical insurance, she can apply for Medicaid.
- Make sure that all legal expenses are documented. Question any expenses that are unclear or that seem unreasonable to you.
- Choose a birthmother who lives at home with her family. This can cut down considerably on the living expenses for which you are responsible. You can also make living arrangements for your birthmother if she agrees.

We are confused as to what we are legally allowed to pay in covering adoption expenses. What expenses are legal?
The Adoption Resource Book by Lois Gilman lists seven expenses you should be expected to pay and seven additional expenses that sometimes come up. The seven expenses that you are expected to pay may vary according to state law:

1. The birthmother's hospital and doctor bills
2. The birthmother's lab fees, vitamins, tests, and drug bills
3. The infant's hospital and pediatric bills
4. The infant's drug bills
5. Counseling for the birthparents
6. Your attorney's fees
7. The birthparents' attorney's fees

Additional expenses you may encounter:

1. The birthmother's lodging and maintenance expenses for one or several months
2. The birthmother's or birthfather's travel expenses if he or she must travel for the surrender of the child
3. Long-distance phone calls
4. The putative father's pregnancy-related expenses (which may include the cost of genetic testing to prove paternity and any financial care or support he provided for the birthmother)
5. Postage for mailing out your résumé
6. Advertising expenses in several newspapers and magazines for several months
7. The installation of a separate phone for your adoption search

Interstate adoptions may involve further costs. You should anticipate the expense of several trips to the state in which the child lives. There also may be additional home study agency costs, attorney fees, and court costs. The adoption procedure varies from state to state; your attorney should assist you in estimating the total adoption expenses as early in the process as possible.

We would like to adopt privately but have limited finances. Can we adopt without using an attorney?
A couple may find the birthparents and work closely with them throughout the adoption process if they choose. However, a competent attorney who is familiar with private adoptions and who knows your state adoption laws is necessary. Private adoption can be successful only when the adoption laws have been strictly adhered to.

We've agreed to pay all medical costs of the birthmother. What do these costs include?
The medical costs of a pregnancy include prenatal care, delivery and hospital fees, prescription medicines taken during the pregnancy, lab tests, blood work, and diagnostic ultrasound scans. Counseling and psychotherapy may also be included. The need for a cesarean section will add to the cost considerably. Always allow for any unforeseen costs when deciding how much you can spend on a private adoption.

We have spent several thousands of dollars on the birthmother's medical expenses. Will we be able to recover any of our money if she changes her mind and stops the adoption before surrendering her rights?
It is very hard to recover any monies you may pay out in medical expenses. We recommend that you discuss this matter with your attorney early in the process. The attorney can prepare a contract to be signed by you and the birthmother,

in which she agrees to repay you for these expenses in the event that she stops the adoption at any time in the process. Be aware that young birthmothers may not have the means to repay such expenses.

Are any of the expenses of an adoption tax deductible?
Yes. You will classify your child as a dependent on your income tax return. You should also be able to claim medical and dental care that the child received while under your care or guardianship. It may be possible to deduct child care if both you and your spouse work. Some states allow portions of the adoption expenses to be deducted.

Legal Considerations

Is private adoption legal?
Private adoption is legal in most—but not all—states. The states in which it is legal have specific guidelines that must be followed to ensure that the adoption is completed legally. Before beginning a private adoption, contact your state child welfare services to determine what is legal and what is not. An attorney who is an expert in the adoption field will answer your legal questions.

What states consider private adoption illegal?
Currently five states require a licensed or state adoption agency to place children in adoptive homes. They are Connecticut, Delaware, Massachusetts, Michigan, and Minnesota.

Are there any options that an adoptive couple may take if they want to adopt privately in a state in which it is illegal?
Yes. Connecticut, Massachusetts, and Minnesota will allow a couple to petition the courts to waive (remove) the agency placement requirement, thus legalizing that private adoption.

**It is illegal to adopt privately in our state. We have had
contact with a birthmother. Will we be able to complete
this adoption?**

Yes. There is an option for couples living in a state requiring
agency placement and supervision of a child placed for
adoption. A couple must contact a licensed adoption agency
that is willing to work with an identified adoption.

What is an identified adoption?

An identified adoption is one in which the birthparents and
the adoptive couple locate each other and then use the
services of an adoption agency. The agency becomes the
mediator, offering the full range of its services to the birthparents
and the adoptive parents. All legal aspects of the adoption
are handled by the agency, thus fulfilling the state requirements.

**Our attorney told us he will need to try to get a prebirth
consent form signed by the birthmother. What kind of form
is this?**

A prebirth consent form is a legal document signed by the
birthparents prior to the birth of their baby. This document
allows the birthparents to surrender all parental and legal
rights to the child. You need to be cautious concerning this
type of document. Have your attorney investigate it thoroughly
to determine if such a document actually terminates parental
rights when signed prior to the baby's birth. This will vary
from state to state.

Do all states allow prebirth consents?

No. Twenty-three states currently prohibit prebirth consents:

Alaska	California	Delaware
Arkansas	Colorado	Florida

Georgia	New Jersey	Tennessee
Indiana	New York	Texas
Maryland	North Carolina	Utah
Minnesota	North Dakota	Vermont
Missouri	Oklahoma	Wyoming
Montana	South Carolina	

Why are prebirth consents prohibited in so many states?
The states prohibiting prebirth consents began their policies in the hope of preventing undue pressure placed on the birthparents to surrender their parental rights.

Which states allow the birthmother to sign a prebirth consent?
Alabama, Hawaii, Washington, and Wisconsin allow prebirth consents. There are no specific laws concerning prebirth consents in the other twenty-three states that do not prohibit such documents.

We have heard that birthparents have to surrender their rights to the child they are giving up for adoption. How do they do this?
The birthparents must sign surrender papers (also called relinquishment papers). These are legal papers that the birthparents voluntarily sign, surrendering all legal and parental rights to the child. The adoptive parents' attorney is responsible for obtaining the signatures. Some states require that the surrender be done before a judge; other states allow the birthparents to sign before a notary public.

Our lawyer said we need a Consent to Adopt paper. What is it?
The Consent to Adopt is another name for the surrender

paper. It is the legal document consenting to the adoption of a child. The Consent to Adopt must be in writing and witnessed, notarized, or executed before a judge or designated official.

Who is legally required to sign the Consent to Adopt (surrender) paper?
Those required to sign may be one or a combination of the following (depending on your state's law):

- The biological mother
- The biological father if
  - He was married to the biological mother at the time of the conception or birth
  - He is named on the birth certificate as the natural father and does not contest it
- The legal or court-appointed guardian of the child
- The child being adopted, if he or she is twelve to fourteen years of age; this requirement varies from state to state
- A parent or court-appointed guardian of the biological parent, if the biological parent is a minor (required in seven states)

After the birthparents sign the surrender papers, can they legally change their minds?
Yes. They legally have the right to change their minds. All states grant birthparents a revocation or waiting period in which they can change their minds and stop the adoption process. This is one reason why adoption can be emotionally stressful.

What happens if our birthmother disappears after the baby's birth? Can exceptions be made as to who signs the Consent to Adopt paper?

Yes. The majority of states allow exceptions in who signs the Consent to Adopt paper in these cases:

- The biological parent has deserted or abandoned the child
- The biological parent is deceased (in which case only a copy of the death certificate is needed)
- The biological parent doesn't have custody of the child, doesn't visit or communicate with the child, and doesn't financially support the child. The classification of abandonment can vary among states from four months to a year
- The biological parent has given up his or her child to an adoption or child-placement agency
- All the parental rights of the biological parent have been legally terminated by the courts
- The biological parent has been declared mentally incompetent
- The biological parent refuses to respond or unreasonably withholds the request to consent
- The biological father is not married to the biological mother

Which states require the parent or guardian of a minor birthparent to sign the Consent to Adopt paper?
Alabama, Indiana, Michigan, Minnesota, New Hampshire, Oklahoma, and Wisconsin.

What does the phrase *revocation of an adoption* mean?
After the birthparents have surrendered their parental rights, they are allowed by their state a specific amount of time to reconsider their adoption decision and to stop the adoption process.

We heard a story on the news about a birthmother who signed surrender papers before the "waiting period" was completed. The birthmother is now challenging the adoption. We do not want this to happen to us. How long is the legal waiting period?

Currently seventeen states require a birthmother to wait a specific amount of time following the birth of her baby before she can legally surrender her parental rights and consent to the adoption. Each state views its allotted amount of time as sufficient for the birthmother to make her adoption decision.

Arizona	4 days	Nevada	4 days
Connecticut	2 days	New Hampshire	4 days
Illinois	4 days	New Mexico	4 days
Iowa	4 days	Ohio	4 days
Kansas	12 hours	Pennsylvania	4 days
Kentucky	6 days	South Dakota	4 days
Louisiana	4 days	Washington, D.C.	4 days
Massachusetts	4 days	West Virginia	4 days
Mississippi	2 days		

After signing the surrender papers, birthparents in all states are given time to change their minds. Ask your attorney to fully explain these statutory provisions. A good understanding of your state's law will help you avoid a very stressful situation should the birthmother change her mind about the surrender. Depending on your state's law, the revocation period may be shortened or waived.

Our attorney told us that during the adoption process he will file an adoption petition. What is an adoption petition?
An adoption petition is the first legal document to be filed in court. This document actually begins the adoption process.

What paperwork is needed for an adoption petition?
This depends on your state law. Typically, the following is required:

- The names, ages, and address of the adoptive parents
- Whether or not any relationship exists between the adoptive parents and the child to be adopted, such as aunt, uncle, or stepparent
- The legal reason why the birthparents' rights are being terminated. Either the rights are given up voluntarily or the birthparents are deemed unfit by the courts
- A written statement that the adoption is in the best interest of the child
- A written statement describing the adoptive parents' suitability to adopt and their ability to provide financially for the child
- The date when the adoptive parents acquired custody of the child and from whom they received custody
- The birth certificate of the child or the birth date and place of birth

We have heard stories in the news about adopted children being taken from their adoptive homes after the adoption was completed. Is this becoming more of a problem for adoptive families?
Several adoption disruption cases have received national media attention. This intense focus on adoption disruptions may leave many prospective adoptive parents fearful of the adoption process. No parent wants to risk loving and caring for a child only to have that child taken from them. Currently there are no statistics on the number of adoptions nationwide that end with the removal of an adopted child from the adoptive home. However, these occurrences are relatively rare.

How can we protect ourselves and make sure that our adoption does not end with a disruption?

We cannot stress frequently enough the importance of strictly adhering to all the adoption laws of your state. It is vital that you hire an attorney with a sound background in adoption law. A questionable adoption will only pave the way for possible troubles in the future. Today prospective adoptive parents are strongly encouraged to register the name of the adoptive child's birthfather (if his identity is known) with the Registry of Unwed Fathers.

There is so much in the news today about the rights of birthparents. What about the rights of the adopted children and their adoptive families whose homes and lives are being destroyed? Who is going to protect their rights?

Don't be discouraged. We, along with millions of American viewers, watched in silent horror as a toddler was pulled kicking and screaming, by a policewoman, from the arms of her adoptive parents. Her crying pleas for the only father she had ever known wrenched our hearts. There was a subsequent outpouring of concern for the rights of adopted children across the country. As a result of this concern, people are demanding better adoption laws to protect those who cannot protect themselves. Tennessee and Michigan are among the states currently reviewing and rewriting their adoption laws. The new laws are intended to protect the rights of adopted children and their adoptive families without sacrificing the rights of the birthparents.

The adoption process seems so complicated. What legally must be done before the adoption takes place?

Before the final adoption hearing, all parental rights of the birthparents must have been terminated. Some judges require a Certificate of Service, showing that the birthmother has been sent a notice of the upcoming hearing. If the legal rights to a child have been surrendered, no Certificate of Service may be necessary. Ask your attorney to provide a step-by-step guide explaining the legal adoption process in your state while he or she keeps you informed of the progress of your adoption.

What is a Certificate of Service?

This is a prior notice of an upcoming adoption hearing and must be given to all persons who are legally required to consent to the adoption. The person or persons being notified must be given thirty days to respond.

How do you notify the appropriate persons about an upcoming adoption hearing?

Notification may be given in any of the following ways:

- By direct contact (in person). Notification should always be in writing
- By letter through the mail, showing a Certificate of Service
- Through public notices in newspapers—but only if you do not know how to reach the person

If the birthmother delivers a child with a disability that we are unable to cope with, are we legally required to complete the adoption?

No. It is important from the beginning to know your limits both financially and emotionally. Determine before the birth any possible medical complications that you can or cannot cope with. Both you and the birthmother are permitted to change your minds about the adoption before it becomes final. By the time of the delivery, a bond may have been formed between you and the birthmother. Try not to abandon her if you decide you cannot adopt the baby. You may be able to help her find someone who can. There are waiting lists for special-needs infants. A good alternate home may be found.

If our child is born with a physical defect, requires extensive hospitalization, or dies before or after the surrender hearing, are we financially liable for the expenses?
The answer to this question depends on your state's law. Whether or not you will be financially liable can also depend on whether you have made any contractual agreements (written or oral) with the birthparents concerning these matters prior to the birth of the child. In private adoption, the adoptive parents are generally required to sign some form of agreement binding them to these financial obligations. If the prospective adoptive parents have not yet signed such an agreement, they will probably not be held responsible for these costs. Your attorney should closely review the pertinent state laws under these circumstances. This is one of the reasons why it is so important to involve a good adoption attorney in your adoption.

Do the baby's biological grandparents have any legal rights regarding the adoption?
Although the grandparents have no legal rights to a child placed for adoption, they may have a great deal of influence over the birthparents. If they are concerned or unhappy with the adoption process, they may try to convince the birthmother or birthfather to stop the adoption. In a situation such as this, adoption counseling that includes the grandparents may serve to resolve any conflicts or concerns, thereby allowing the adoption to proceed.

We have heard of birthmothers changing their minds and taking a baby right out of the adoptive couple's home. How long will it take after we bring the baby home before the child will be legally ours?

Ask your attorney what your individual state legally requires. The time allotted for a birthmother to change her mind and take back her child varies. In some states, such as Hawaii, a child cannot be taken from an adoptive home after being placed in that home, unless it is in the best interest of the child. In other states, such as Maryland, the birthmother has ninety days or until the final adoption decree to change her mind—whichever comes first. After the revocation period has ended, the birthparents' parental rights are terminated. State laws vary on the length of time after the adoption petition is filed until the final hearing when the child is legally yours.

How does the adoption of twins differ from that of a single birth?

Some states may require separate paperwork (documentation, petitions for adoption, and final decrees) for each child's adoption, but the adoptions take place at the same time.

Is it a common practice for twins to be placed in separate adoptive homes?

In the past, when adoptive homes were scarce, twins and sibling groups were placed in separate adoptive homes. The trend today is to place twins and sibling groups together. Twin and sibling group placements of two young, healthy children may not be considered special-needs placement. Sibling groups of three or more always constitute a special-needs adoption.

We talked with an attorney about private adoption, and he told us we will need state approval. What does this mean?

Your attorney is referring to your state's guidelines mandating the screening of a prospective adoptive couple's suitability as parents. This means you will be required to have a home study completed before the adoption can be finalized. Suitability will be determined through an extensive study of your home environment and family life. *Note:* For more details see the section "The Home Study" in the chapter titled "Agency Adoption."

Considerations Regarding Attorneys

Our friends adopted a child last year, and they had to pay two attorneys. Why?

Some states require that a birthmother be represented by an attorney separate from that of the adoptive couple. This is to prevent a conflict of interest. In the case of two attorneys, the adoptive couple is required to pay the fees of both parties for services rendered.

Do attorneys have a set fee for private adoption?

Most do not, because there are too many variables with each adoption.

Do attorneys keep waiting lists of prospective adoptive parents?

Many attorneys who handle private adoptions maintain a waiting list or files on prospective adoptive parents. Frequently these files contain résumés or "Dear Birthmother" letters with pictures and biographical data. They use these files when birthparents contact them. You should contact the attorney before sending such information to him or her.

Birthfathers

Do unwed fathers have any legal rights to their biological children?

Yes. An unwed father, also known as the putative father, has full legal rights to obtain custody of his child. He has the right to consent to or prevent an adoption. An unwed father must establish his paternity before he can exercise any rights to the child.

How does an unwed father establish his paternity?

There are four steps that a man must take if he wants to establish the legal paternity of a child:

1. He must have his name submitted to the State Registry of Vital Statistics, or to the Registry of Unwed Fathers.
2. He must acknowledge the child by signing the birth certificate.
3. He must act the role of father by actually caring for the child's physical needs, financially supporting the child, or communicating with the child.
4. He must present his case and obtain a court order establishing his paternity.

What happens if we locate a birthmother who says she doesn't know who the birthfather is? Can we still legally adopt her baby?

It is important to know the name and whereabouts of the birthfather if at all possible, so he can sign the Consent to Adopt papers or deny his paternity. This prevents future legal problems. It is up to the birthmother to decide whether to list the birthfather on the birth certificate. If the birthmother is not married to the birthfather, the only way a birthfather's name will appear on the birth certificate is for him to be present at the hospital and sign the record of birth. If the birthfather does not take steps to earn his right as the biological father before the petition for adoption takes place, he usually will not try to seek or exert parental rights once the adoption is underway. *Beware:* Sometimes a birthfather finds out later that he is the father of a child being adopted, and he can intervene by establishing his paternity. It is then up to the court to decide if the adoption is in the best interest of the child.

Adoption Laws

Where can we get a copy of our state's adoption laws?
The main library in your town may have a copy of your state's laws. If it doesn't, ask the librarian to get it for you. Keep in mind that these laws are in legal language and may be hard to understand. The National Adoption Information Clearinghouse can provide you with a comprehensive book on adoption laws that is easy to read and follow. The book covers general adoption requirements and a summary of state-by-state laws. The cost of the book is ten dollars. To order a copy, write to the following address:

Adoption Laws: Answers to the Most Asked
   Questions
National Adoption Information Clearinghouse
Suite 410
11426 Rockville Pike
Rockville, MD 20852
(301) 231-6512

Locating a Baby

We have no idea where we can locate a baby. Where do we start?

Everyone you meet is a potential contact in locating a birthmother. Follow these steps:

- Have a separate phone with an unlisted number installed in your home for birthmothers to call
- Develop a résumé and a "Dear Birthmother" letter to give to potential contacts who may help you locate your birthmother
- Have your first name, telephone number, and the fact that you want to adopt a child printed on cards to hand out and leave in laundromats, on bulletin boards, and in other public places. Give several to everyone you know, and ask these people to pass them out to their friends
- Advertise in local papers, magazines, flyers, and specialty advertising supplements. Check with your attorney first to see if advertising is legal in your state
- Contact the following:
  Physicians
  Attorneys
  Adoptive parent support groups
  Free clinics, such as Planned Parenthood, birth-control institutes, and women's clinics
  Ministers, priests, and rabbis
  Local middle school and high school counselors
  Colleges
  Friends, neighbors, and people that you meet daily

Remember: The more you advertise and spread the word, the more responses you will get. The next call could be that special birthmother!

How do we write a résumé that will interest a birthmother enough to contact us?

Make your résumé a personal letter. Tell the birthmother about yourself and your family and your desires, wishes, hopes, and dreams for a child. Birthmothers like to know that the potential adoptive parents are "real" people. Briefly describe your family, home, neighborhood, employment, church, vacations, and interests.

My parents said their neighbors used an intermediary when they adopted. What is an intermediary?

An intermediary is a person working to bring the birthparents and adoptive parents together. Doctors, attorneys, teachers, health-care professionals, friends, and relatives can all be intermediaries. The intermediary is not paid for locating an infant. Currently, in twenty states it is illegal to pay an intermediary. Check with your attorney about your state laws.

We have heard that newspaper adoption ads can be very successful. We would like to try placing our own ad. How do we go about writing a successful ad?

Plan your ad carefully. In as few words as possible, explain to the potential birthmother why you want to adopt a child and how loved and cared for the child will be. Remember that you are trying to convince someone to let you raise her child. You will want to project warmth and sincerity. Imagine yourself in the birthmother's position. What kind of ad would you find attractive enough to place your child with a couple? *Note:* Ads for adoption are illegal in some states.

Black- and Gray-Market Adoptions

Can you explain the difference between a gray-market adoption, a black-market adoption, and a legal adoption?
The birthmother receives some financial support in all of these adoptions. It is the amount of money or what the money is used for that determines whether the adoption is legal.

Adoptive parents are allowed to pay for the medical and living expenses of the birthmother (rent, utilities, medical care, food, and clothes).

In a *gray-market adoption*, the adoptive parents give questionable financial assistance to the birthmother. Designer clothes, college tuition, a new vehicle, rent for a luxury condominium, and reimbursement for elective sterilization following the delivery of the baby can fall into the category of a gray-market adoption.

In a *black-market adoption*, large sums of money are given to the birthmother to ensure she signs the Consent to Adopt paper. The money may be given under the guise of living expenses and legal fees the birthmother owes.

There are no circumstances under which "buying" a baby would be morally or legally right. Do not let your desire for a baby lead you into a black-market adoption. Patience and perseverance will bring you your special birthmother and baby.

What expenses are illegal to pay during a private adoption?
Ask your attorney to explain what adoption expenses are illegal in your state. It is a felony to buy and sell children. To prevent getting mixed up in a black-market adoption, carefully avoid any payment to the birthmother that is not specifically authorized by state law. Do not give the birthmother cash gifts, bonds, or large ticket items, such as deeds to property or cars.

Religious Considerations

Are birthparents and adoptive parents required to be of the same religion in a private adoption?
In some states the birthparents and adoptive parents are required to be of the same religious faith. In those states there have been couples who have successfully petitioned the courts for a waiver of such laws when the birthmother had no religious preference.

Choosing a Physician

Who chooses the obstetrician and pediatrician?
The birthmother may choose her own OB/GYN. If she is uncertain, you may want to suggest a physician who will provide her with sound medical care and emotional support of her adoption decision. The adoptive parents choose the pediatrician for the child.

Counseling

Is psychological counseling required for the birthmother?
In some states psychological counseling for the birthmother is required. This allows her to carefully weigh her decision to place the child for adoption. It may prevent a birthmother from changing her mind by giving her confidence that she is making the right choice. She will be better prepared to face the separation from her child.

How much counseling should a birthmother receive?
The amount of counseling a birthmother requires is different for each individual. A birthmother who has previously placed one or more children will require less than a teenager who is unprepared for the stress of pregnancy and birth. Ask the

counselor for an initial assessment of the amount of counseling that may be needed. If your funds are limited, emphasize to the counselor the budget that you must work within while assuring that the birthmother receives the help she needs.

Who arranges counseling for the birthmother?
Your physician or attorney may know of a person who specializes in adoption counseling. You may choose to call an adoption agency and request that their counselor see the birthmother. When choosing a counselor from an agency, be sure to select one who views private adoption as a positive way to adopt a child.

Medical Concerns

We recently discovered that our birthmother has taken an antidepressant throughout her pregnancy. How can we determine any possible effect it will have on the baby?
Request the name and dosage of any medication that you find out the birthmother is taking. Contact your pharmacist to locate the name and customer service number of the company producing the drug. The drug company will have a representative who is able to discuss your questions concerning prenatal exposure to the medication. Ask your doctor. He or she should be willing to talk to you about any side effects the drug may have on the unborn child. Most birthmothers will sign a medical authorization form that gives your attorney the right to request the birthmother's medical records. Ask your attorney to discuss any medication such as antidepressants with the birthmother's physician.

What type and how much medical history will we be able to obtain from the birthparents?

All states require the birthparents to fill out background information forms, which include some medical history. In most states extensive medical background information is required from both the birthmother and the birthfather (if his identity is known).

Once the baby is born, who makes the medical decisions for the child—the birthmother or the adoptive parents?
The birthmother makes all the medical decisions that arise while she is still in the hospital. The only time that a birthmother needs to sign a medical authorization or consent form is when the adoptive parents take the child out of the hospital before the surrender hearing. Once the surrender hearing has taken place, the adoptive parents make any and all medical decisions.

Interstate Adoption

What does *interstate adoption* mean?
Interstate adoption simply means that the child is a resident of one state, and the adoptive parents live in another state.

If we locate a birthmother in another state, will we be required to travel to that state?
Yes, you will have to travel to the state in which the baby was born to bring home the baby. Many states require for the surrender hearing that you go to court with the birthparents in the state where they reside. Generally, the adoptive parents travel to the state where the child is located and obtain legal custody there. The child is then taken to the adoptive parents' state, where the petition for adoption is filed. The laws in your state and in the other state should be checked on as early as possible during the adoption process. Either an

attorney or an agency in each state should be involved. However, interstate adoptions are common, and you should not shy away from them if the right match is found.

Our attorney told us that if we locate a birthmother in another state we must adhere to the Interstate Compact. What is this?

The Interstate Compact on the Placement of Children is a statute that has been adopted by all states to standardize and simplify the procedure by which a child living in one state can be adopted in another state. In every state, specific guidelines have to be followed and adhered to before the baby can be legally taken from one state to another. A birthmother must initiate the adoption procedures by signing a 100A Form. This signed form, as well as other required documents, must be filed by the birthmother's attorney with the Interstate Compact office. Prospective adoptive parents must file their home study with the Interstate Compact office in their state. Each state's office exchanges information with the other state involved. The Interstate Compact office must give approval before the baby can be moved to another state. Each state has an Interstate Compact coordinator with whom the prospective adoptive parents will work closely.

The Birth Certificate

What information will our adopted child's birth certificate contain?

Your adopted child will have two birth certificates. The original birth certificate will list the birthmother and birthfather (if his identity is known) as the child's parents, and will identify the child's place of birth. The child is usually named by the birthmother. In the event your birthmother doesn't choose a first name for the child, the adoptive parents will be asked to choose a temporary name for the child's original birth certificate. This name can be legally changed at the adoption finalization. The second birth certificate is issued at the adoption finalization. This birth certificate contains the child's new adoptive name, date of birth, sex, and the names of the adoptive parents as the natural parents. A copy of the original birth certificate is kept in the sealed court adoption records.

Financial Aid

Where can we find financial aid to help with the costs of our adoption?
There are two possible sources for adoption subsidies or financial aid. Many employers today recognize adoption as a positive way to build a family. These progressive companies will reimburse their employees up to a set amount of money to help offset the costs of adoption. The second source is a government subsidy provided to help with the adoption of special-needs or hard-to-place children.

Will our adopted child be covered by our health insurance as soon as he or she comes to our home?
You must check with your insurance company before your child comes to your home. Some health insurance companies cover only "legally adopted" children, while others start coverage as soon as you initiate legal proceedings. It is important that the insurance company understands that though the child is not "legally" yours upon placement in your home, you are held solely responsible for all the child's needs, including medical needs.

A Summary of the Steps Required in an Independent Adoption

1. Contact the child welfare services in your area to determine if independent (private) adoption is legal in your state.
2. If at all possible, choose an adoption attorney before you locate a birthmother.
3. Prepare a list of specific adoption questions and schedule an appointment with your adoption attorney.
4. Install a separate phone line in your home, contact intermediaries, and advertise.
5. Make a list of the questions you want to discuss with a potential birthmother. For example: What are your needs for this adoption? How can we make your adoption plans easier for you as a birthmother? Would you like to talk with an adoption counselor or social worker about your adoption decision? How much contact do you expect to have with the adoptive family before and after the adoption? These questions can be discussed in an initial phone call with the birthmother, or your attorney can handle the initial interview with the birthparents.
6. Determine what medical and pregnancy expenses will be paid to the birthmother, and have the monetary transactions between yourself and the birthparents handled through the adoption attorney. Document all expenses.
7. Locate an adoption agency or social worker who can complete your home study and provide professional counseling for the birth family if needed.
8. Complete your home study. Gather the necessary documents such as marriage certificates, birth certificates, financial statements, and personal references. Also, be sure that each member of your household is given (or has recently been given) a complete medical examination.

9. Obtain medical insurance coverage for your adoptive infant prior to the birth.
10. Attend the surrender hearing.
11. Take your infant home. You may take your infant home prior to the surrender hearing if you are accepting a legal risk placement.
12. File the Petition to Adopt forms.
13. Legally finalize your adoption through the courts in a timely manner.

Chapter 5

INTERNATIONAL ADOPTION

*I*nternational adoption is a popular and viable way to build a family. The number of foreign adoptions has continued to grow over the past few years, despite stories of the process being lengthy and costly. International adoption is an alternative to the long waiting lists and restrictions that adoptive families may face when trying to adopt a healthy infant here in the United States. Hundreds of thousands of abandoned children around the world wait in orphanages, institutions, and refugee camps for families of their own. Why are so many children abandoned in foreign countries every year? The number one reason is poverty, followed by changing world governments, natural disasters, war, and illegitimacy. Many times these children will continue to live in appalling conditions and may never live to see adulthood. Adoptive homes offer these children a chance for survival.

International adoption is an exciting option for

many people—particularly for those who want to adopt infants, for families with children, for singles wanting to adopt, and for those prospective parents who do not meet the U.S. adoption agency requirements. As you consider international adoption, keep in mind that the process is complex, frustrating, and ever changing, and that it can become expensive. However, international adoption can be rewarding and satisfying. Many international adoptions have been completed more quickly and have cost less than stateside adoptions.

Deciding If International Adoption Is for You

What are some things we should consider before deciding if international adoption is for us?
Consider these questions and facts carefully and truthfully to see if you should pursue international adoption:

- What characteristics do you expect your child to have? Do you understand that your child will be of a separate race or nationality and may look different from you? How will you deal with this?
- Will you be willing to help your child understand his or her heritage and have a sense of personal identity? Will you be willing to help your child learn about his or her culture if your child shows an interest?
- What are your true motives for adopting an international child? Do you feel that you will be doing a good deed if you save a poor, homeless child?
- How do you feel about the probability of becoming an interracial family? Your family will be interracial for generations to come.

- How do you feel about interracial dating and marriage? Your child will not be a cute little infant forever. How will your friends and neighbors react if your child wants to date one of their children? And how will you feel if your child chooses to marry a person of his or her race or of a different race?
- How will you react when you encounter negative reactions from the public? Some people will think you are in an interracial marriage. Is that OK with you? If your child has different features from yours, you will be questioned everywhere you go—often in front of the child. What will you say to these people so that your child will maintain healthy self-esteem?

Adoption Information

We would like to read about international adoption before we make an adoption decision, but we are having trouble finding information. Where can we turn?
Los Ninos International Adoption Center is a licensed non-profit organization that places children from Bolivia, China, Colombia, Ecuador, Guatemala, Honduras, Peru, the Russian Republic, and the Ukraine. It offers free international adoption information for couples and singles residing in the U.S. or abroad. Send a self-addressed, stamped business envelope and two U.S. postage stamps to:

> Los Ninos "The Children" International Adoption Center
> P.O. Box 9617
> The Woodlands, TX 77380
> (713) 363-2892

For twenty dollars you can also order, from the same address, *How to Adopt Internationally: A Guide for Agency Directed and Independent Adoptions*. This book provides current names, addresses, and telephone numbers of child-placing entities, laws, and procedures in Africa, Asia, Europe, and Latin America. It also examines planning for the expenses, preparing for the trip, caring for the Third World orphan, and much more. This 197-page soft-cover book, updated in 1993, will give you a good overall view of international adoption to help you make your decision.

We want to adopt from a foreign country. Which countries at this time allow Americans to adopt?
Many countries allow international adoption. Keep in mind that political upheaval around the world can cause international adoption laws to change suddenly. Check with the State Department or the Immigration and Naturalization Service in your area. They will tell you whether or not adoptions are allowed in the country in which you are interested. We have provided Immigration Service addresses for you in the chapter titled "Adoption Resources." The following countries allow international adoptions at the time of this writing:

Africa	India
Ethiopia	Japan
Mali	Korea
Niger	Nepal
Uganda	Philippines
	Taiwan
Asia	Thailand
China	Vietnam
Hong Kong	

Europe
- Bulgaria
- Belarus
- Estonia
- Greece
- Hungary
- Latvia
- Moldova
- Poland
- Romania
- Russian Republic
- Ukraine

Latin America
- Bolivia
- Brazil
- Chile
- Colombia
- Costa Rica
- Dominican Republic
- Ecuador
- El Salvador
- Guatemala
- Haiti
- Honduras
- Jamaica
- Mexico
- Nicaragua
- Panama
- Paraguay
- Peru
- Saint Lucia
- Turks and Caicos Islands

If you choose to work with a country that is in a state of political unrest, we suggest you pick an alternate country in the event that adoptions are temporarily suspended in the country of your choice.

The Agency

Once we have chosen a country from which we would like to adopt, how do we locate an agency that will work with us?

We highly recommend that you write for the *Report on Foreign Adoption*. It is published yearly and updated monthly by the International Concerns Committee for Children. At present the *Report* is the only nationwide resource in the

U.S. and Canada to which prospective adoptive parents and adoption agencies can turn for updated information. This thorough report covers every country that allows international adoption and the U.S. agencies that work with each country. Each agency is listed with the age and type of children available, the time estimated for placement of a child in your home, the cost of the adoption, travel requirements, and whether it accepts applications from single people. The report also includes the health regulations for foreign countries, medical information, adjustments to expect a child from a foreign country to make, and helpful facts that will guide you to make an informed decision. You will receive monthly updates. For the *Report on Foreign Adoption* send a donation of twenty dollars to the following address:

> International Concerns Committee For Children
> 911 Cypress Drive
> Boulder, CO 80303
> (303) 494-8333

Several agencies in our state place children from the country we are interested in. How do we go about choosing the agency that is right for us?

- Call each agency and ask what services they offer and which countries they work with.
- Find out if the agency conducts its own home studies.
- Ask about the requirements for adoptive parents—such as age, previous divorces, religion, infertility, income, and U.S. citizenship—and also about the requirements of the child's country of origin.
- Ask for an outline of the agency's fee structure: the application fee (usually nonrefundable); the home-study, document-processing, and translation fees; international

program and processing fees; I.N.S. fees; and travel expenses for you and your child. Does the agency have an installment payment plan?

- Do they provide orientation meetings? Attend as many agency orientation meetings as possible before you decide which agency you want to work with.
- Ask for references. Talk with other adoptive parents about their experiences. This is a very important step!
Adoptive parents love to tell about every aspect of their experience and can be very candid about the positive and negative sides to adoption.
- Obtain outside information about the agency. Contact the child welfare office in your state to find out if the agency you are interested in has been certified by the state. Talk to various adoption support groups in your area. They will be a valuable resource about adoption agencies.
- Apply to the one agency of your choice. You should work with only one agency at a time.

State Requirements

Do all states allow international adoption? Whom do we check with about the laws of our state?

Many states require that an international adoption be an identified adoption. This means that a specific child in another country is located, and his or her name is known before the adoption process can start. You can obtain free information about the laws governing international adoption in your state through your local Department of Child Welfare Services. Ask to speak with the person who handles international adoptions for that office. That person will have the most up-to-date information concerning international adoptions in your state. Some states require that adoptive parents seek approval for their international adoption through the Office of Interstate Adoption. In this case your home study must be submitted to this office for state approval before traveling to adopt. A copy of the approval will be sent to Immigrations.

Immigrations Requirements

After we have applied to work with an agency and have begun the waiting process, is there anything we can do to help speed up our adoption process?
Yes. Call your closest I.N.S. office and ask them to send you an I-600A Form (Application for Advance Processing of an Orphan Petition). You will be required to send the following:

- Proof that you are a United States citizen. This can be your birth certificate or your current passport
- Proof of marriage
- Proof of termination of any previous marriages (divorce decree)
- A favorably recommended home study. If your home study is not yet completed, go ahead and send in the application, fee, and any other requirements. The home study must be submitted within one year of your completion of the Advance Processing application, or the application will be considered abandoned
- A nonrefundable application fee. This is currently $140 but can increase without notice
- Two sets each of the fingerprint cards (Form FD-258) that the Immigrations office sends with your application. These can be done by your local law enforcement agency or volunteer organization free of charge
- A letter of your state's approval, if required by your state.

This letter can be obtained from your state's Interstate Compact Office

The agency we have decided to work with said they will not be able to start our home study for a few months. Do we need to hold on to the I-600A form until the home study is completed?
You can fill out the application and send in the fingerprint cards before your home study is completed. It will help to speed the approval process. The fingerprint cards are sent from Immigrations to the FBI for processing. This process can take up to two months. The I.N.S. will open a file in your name and wait until the arrival of your home-study report before final approval. From the time Immigrations receives your home-study report it will be only a matter of days before you are approved by Immigrations (if you have been cleared by the FBI).

My husband and I have never been arrested. Why does Immigrations require us to have a fingerprint check?
The fingerprint check determines whether either of the prospective adoptive parents has ever been arrested or convicted; and if convicted, the number of convictions, the nature of the offense, and whether the individual is considered to be rehabilitated. The I.N.S. is looking especially for any drug-related convictions or sexual abuse convictions that potentially would put a child at risk. All of these factors are considered in determining whether the prospective adoptive parents will be able to properly care for a child.

Why does it take up to two months for the FBI to clear our fingerprints if we have never had a criminal record?
It is the policy of Immigrations to expedite all orphan cases

for humanitarian reasons. The fingerprint forms sent to FBI headquarters for a criminal record search can take up to two months. That is why prospective adoptive parents are encouraged to use the advance processing procedures.

Once we receive approval by the I.N.S. for an international adoption, do we complete the adoption by traveling immediately to the country where our child lives?
You must have I.N.S. approval before you can complete an international adoption. I.N.S. approval is valid for one year from the date it is issued. Adoptive parents can travel at any time during that year to complete their international adoption.

How will we know when we are approved by Immigrations?
Once Immigrations has reached a decision of approval, you will receive in the mail Form I-171H, which is the Notice of Favorable Determination Concerning Application for Advance Processing of Orphan Petition. This decision does not guarantee that the orphan petition you later file on behalf of a child will be approved unless the child qualifies as an orphan under U.S. law. If your Advance Processing application is denied, you have the right to appeal.

I know of a very poor family in Brazil with ten children. They want to find an American family to adopt their three-year-old. Even with the extreme poverty and difficult circumstances, does this child have to be considered an orphan in order for us to adopt her?
For an adopted foreign child to be brought into the U.S., Immigrations requires that the child be classified as an orphan. Under immigration law an orphan is defined as follows:

> A foreign child who has *no parents* because of the death or disappearance of, abandonment or desertion by, or

separation or loss from both parents. An orphan is also a foreign child with *only one parent* who is not able to take care of the child properly and has in writing forever or *irrevocably released* the orphan for emigration and adoption.

An orphan petition must be filed before the child's sixteenth birthday. An orphan can be denied immigration to the U.S. for health reasons, such as a contagious disease, AIDS, or other problems. Based on the preceding guidelines, an immigrant visa will not be issued to the three-year-old child because she cannot be classified as an orphan by the U.S. government.

Once our adopted child has a visa, will he or she be considered an American citizen?
When an orphan enters the U.S. with an immigrant visa, the orphan is considered to be a lawful, permanent resident of the U.S., but not a U.S. citizen. You will receive a legal alien card for your child to carry until he or she becomes a U.S. citizen.

We are pursuing an international adoption. Who keeps the I.N.S. approval forms—the adoptive parents or the adoption agency?
Once you are approved to adopt internationally, the I.N.S. will send you Form I-171H titled Notice of Favorable Determination Concerning Application for Advance Processing of Orphan Petition. You will give a copy of this document to the adoption agency you are working with, and you will keep the original. It is important that you take this document with you to the country in which you are adopting. The U.S. Embassy will need this document before your adopted child's immigration visa can be given. For example, if you are adopting a child from a Romanian orphanage, the adoption agency in the U.S. will have a copy of the I.N.S. document. You will

keep the original and take it to the U.S. Embassy in Bucharest to receive your child's immigration visa into the U.S.

What documents will we need if we have not been preapproved?

Some of the documents that will be required are the following:

- A filing fee (subject to change)
- Proof of your U.S. citizenship
- A copy of your marriage certificate
- Salary statement from your employer
- The child's birth certificate and a Statement of Release of Child for Adoption and Immigration

Note: It is important to be pre-approved by Immigrations if at all possible. Pre-approval will speed up and smooth out the process.

What is an orphan petition?

An orphan petition is a form that is completed for immigration benefits on behalf of a specific child. The child's name, the child's date of birth, and other information about the child must be known before the petition is completed.

Where do we file the orphan petition?

The I-600A Form can be filed at an Immigrations office near you or at the American Consulate or Embassy in the country of the adoption. You will need the following:

- Proof of the orphan's age from the birth certificate or evidence of birth
- The death certificate of the biological parent, if applicable
- Proof that the surviving parent cannot provide support

and proper care, and their consent to adoption and emigration

- A final adoption decree
- Abandonment papers from the orphanage
- Proof that all preadoption requirements have been met by the state of the orphan's proposed residence
- A favorable decision in a completed Advance Processing application
- Proof that you and your spouse or you as a single individual personally saw the child prior to the adoption. In the case of a married couple, if the child was not seen by both adoptive parents prior to the adoption, U.S. law requires that the child be readopted when you return to the U.S. *Note:* The orphan petition is the final step to be completed by you before leaving for the U.S. with your adoptive child.

Choosing a Child

We have no children, and my husband really wants a boy. I am afraid many people ask to adopt boys. If we request a boy, will we have a longer wait? What should we do?
Actually, wanting to adopt a boy puts you in the minority among prospective adoptive parents. Most adoption agencies receive many more applications requesting girls than those requesting boys. This is true whether the family wants an infant or an older child. The adoption process will be easier if you are willing to take a child of either sex. The foreign agency will be able to give you the next available baby or help you choose a child from waiting children.

What types of children are available for adoption in foreign countries?
Children born in foreign countries who are available for

adoption come in many skin colors and vary in ages from newborn to teenagers. They can have varying degrees of handicaps. Most come from poor families in which the birth-mother received poor or no prenatal care, and they have experienced early neglect, poor health care, and a lack of good nutrition. Some of the health problems you may en-counter include the following:

- Malnutrition
- Parasites
- Minor congenital defects
- Diseases such as tuberculosis and hepatitis B

You will find detailed information on these conditions in the chapter titled "International Medical Considerations".

We want a reasonably healthy child. Will our agency provide us with an in-depth medical history on our child?
Reputable agencies provide prospective adoptive parents with as much information as possible on the child's background and medical history. In some cases you may receive very little information on the medical history and background of the child. Unfortunately, record-keeping in many countries is poor. No agency can guarantee the accuracy and reliability of the information they have been given. Most U.S. adoption agencies work closely with individuals or agencies in the foreign country. Many children overseas have not been immunized, and often the birth families' medical histories are nonexistent. Sometimes in the case of an abandoned child even the child's exact age is not known.

My husband and I have decided we would be willing to adopt a child with a minor disability that can be easily treated or

surgically corrected. We are afraid that if we tell the agency this they might try to give us a child with a more severe handicap. What should we do?

It is very important to be honest with your social worker about the kind of child you are willing to take. The agency wants to bring together a child and a prospective parent who will make a happy and successful family. Agencies will not "force" a child on you that you cannot handle. Agencies should give you a list of conditions and handicaps if they know you are willing to take a special-needs child. This list will contain such conditions as club foot, eye conditions, tuberculosis, diabetes, cleft lip, hyperactivity, speech problems, and delayed development. You will be asked to list which conditions are acceptable to you, along with the severity of each condition. Be honest with yourself and with your social worker about problems that you can and cannot handle. You may be able to adopt a child more quickly if you are willing to accept even a minor handicap.

How will our agency decide which child to place with us? Will we have any say in the decision?

When adopting from a foreign country, you may or may not be placed on a waiting list, because each applicant has individual specifications that may be easier or harder to fill. When the agency has matched a child with you who meets your specifications, the agency will give you some information about the child. Don't be surprised if they do not have a photograph of the child or any detailed medical information. You may be given as little as twenty-four hours to decide whether you will accept that child or not. The agency may tell you of a child who does not exactly meet your requirements, but who they feel you might consider. It will be your choice to determine whether the child they are offering is right for you. Expect the decision to be an emotional one.

The agency we have chosen to work with has pictures of available children for us to choose from. Will we need to be preapproved by the I.N.S. to adopt one of these children?
In all circumstances it is advisable to go ahead and file an Advance Processing form (I-600A) with Immigrations. If you already have the name of the child you will be adopting, you can request the I.N.S. to send you the blue I.N.S. form, I-600. This is called a Petition to Classify Orphan as an Immediate Relative. This document is used to obtain your child's immigrant visa. Your agency can tell you which papers you will need to give to the U.S. Consulate or Embassy in your child's country of origin.

U.S. Immigration Resources

International adoption seems so confusing and overwhelming. Are there any resources to help us better understand U.S. immigration laws?
The I.N.S. publishes a booklet, *Immigration of Adopted and Prospective Adoptive Children,* which contains important and helpful information and all the forms necessary for the immigration adoption approval process. To receive this free booklet, write or call your nearest I.N.S. office. You can find the addresses of all I.N.S. offices in the chapter titled "Adoption Resources." The booklet includes the following information:

- The eligibility and benefits for an orphan who will be immigrating to the U.S
- Basic orphan petition procedures and requirements
- Overseas orphan investigations and difficult issues

- United States citizenship for a foreign-born child
- Laws and forms necessary in adopting a foreign-born child

Compiling Your Dossier

Trying to adopt from a foreign country seems so confusing. How do we begin the process of international adoption?
Compile the documents you will need for your home study, Immigrations, and the document dossier required for completion of the adoption in a foreign court. A list of the documents needed for the home study can be found in the section "The Home Study" in the chapter titled "Agency Adoption." If you are working with an agency, they will tell you which documents are required for the country to which you will be traveling. The following list will give you a general idea of the paperwork you will need. All of these documents must be notarized or certified, and you will need four to six copies of each.

- The birth certificate of both adoptive parents
- Your marriage license, and, if applicable, divorce decrees from any previous marriages
- Copies of current physical exams for members of your family who reside with you, and a letter from your physician stating that you and your spouse are in good health and are not carriers of any communicable diseases (These documents can be obtained from your local public health department to help cut down on cost.)
- Financial statements, including a copy of your last tax return(to verify your salary), statements of assets and liabilities, and letters from your bank describing your accounts and confirming that you are in good standing with that bank

- Letters from your employer(s) confirming your position, your salary, and the length of your employment
- Three to five letters of recommendation from friends, family, and associates
- A police clearance from your local law enforcement agency (They will be happy to do a records and background search for you and will notarize the document in multiple copies at no charge.)
- Psychological evaluations (These are not usually needed, so check with your agency first.)

Will it cost anything to compile these documents? What should we expect to spend?
The cost of compiling these documents can run up to sixty dollars, excluding the cost of the physical exams, but it can be compiled at little or no cost. All documents for the adoption must be translated by a certified translator or a notary from the country in which you will be adopting. This can add three hundred to five hundred dollars to your adoption cost, and is usually included within your total adoption fee charged by your agency. An agency may make additional charges for document handling, messenger services, long-distance phone calls, and mailing costs. Be sure to ask the agency up front for an itemized list of all the expected costs. This can save you much frustration and aggravation later.

Are there ways we can cut down on any of these expenses?
Yes.

- Have your health exams done at a public health department.
- Have a friend or acquaintance who is a notary public notarize your papers. Many notary publics will do this free of charge. To find a notary who may help you, ask your church

office, bank officer, insurance agent, friends, and family. (Make sure the adoption agency will accept that notary public. Some agencies may require you to use their own.)

- Do any of your friends or acquaintances know of a person living in the U.S. who comes from the country to which you will be traveling? Often these people will be willing to translate the documents for you at a rate that is much reduced from what the agency will charge. Check with your local colleges and universities for students who have come from that country, and contact them. Ask the person who plans to notarize your documents if he or she will accept the translations. Ask the person doing the translations to sign a paper in front of the notary, stating that the documents are correct and true. Again, check to see if your agency will allow this.

- Sometimes employees of airlines can send Federal Express packets and packages to a foreign country at a fraction of the cost. Ask your friends if they know of someone willing to mail the documents for you. As you can see, friends and acquaintances can become an important part of your adoption process. Remember—just ask! *Note:* The foreign country in which you are adopting may require all documents translated within their country by a government-certified notary.

After we have completed all the required documents, what do we do with them?

Keep a copy of each document for your files. The foreign country may require the agency (or you) to send these documents and the completed home study to your county clerk, your U.S. Department of State, and the appropriate foreign consulate to be authenticated. All of these documents and their translations are sent to the appropriate foreign institution or contact.

The Process of International Adoption

What is the first step in the actual adoption process when adopting internationally?
The first step, after you have located an adoption agency, is the home study. The process consists of a series of interviews with the social worker, who will help you think more thoroughly about adopting a child and about how you would feel toward a child from a different culture. The social worker will want to make sure you can provide a safe and loving environment for a child. The approved home study will state that you are suitable to adopt and have met all of the agency's requirements. The home study will provide for the foreign courts a description of you (and your spouse, if applicable) and your home.

We want to begin our adoption as soon as possible. How long will it take to complete the home study?
A home study is approved usually in a few months but can take longer, depending on how many applicants the agency is working with at the time. For more information on the home-study process, see the section "The Home Study" in the chapter titled "Agency Adoption."

Cost

We are willing to spend a certain amount of money to adopt but are afraid that international adoption will be too expensive for us. What should we expect to spend for an international adoption?
An international adoption will cost anywhere from six thousand to twenty thousand dollars. You may have to add the cost of travel to these figures. The average international adoption will cost around ten thousand dollars, including

travel. Be aware that international adoption costs can vary greatly depending on the country and the adoption agency. It is important to shop around and compare agency costs. Independent international adoption as well as the adoption of foreign-born children with special needs or of children on an adoption waiting list can save a great deal of money on the overall adoption cost.

Will we have to pay the adoption fee all at once?
No. You will be required to send the agency an initial nonrefundable application fee. Many agencies will prorate their fees by your income, and most will let you pay on an installment plan. You will pay the following:

- The agency's fee, which will include the cost of the home study
- All document fees, including translations
- The fees for services provided by the foreign agency, and other expenses incurred in the foreign country, such as attorney fees and court costs

The Adoption

Once we have accepted the child, what is the next step? Will we be allowed to travel to the foreign country immediately?
Once you have accepted a child, the agency generally will require you to pay the final fee of its installment plan. At that point the adoption process in the foreign country can begin. You may or may not travel at that stage. Adoption in most foreign countries can be lengthy. During this time, you are responsible for the following:

- You may be financially responsible for the cost of the child's foster care and medical expenses during the adoption process. Foster care can be as much as two hundred dollars a month. If the child is in an orphanage or similar institution, he or she will usually remain there (until you arrive to pick up the child) at no cost to you.
- You will have to give a foreign attorney your power of attorney to represent you in court during the adoption proceedings. The fee for this service is usually covered in the foreign fees.
- When the child is legally adopted in the foreign country and you have not been preapproved by the I.N.S., you are required to complete an I-600 Form (Petition to Classify an Orphan as an Immediate Relative) and file it with the I.N.S. When the petition has been approved by the I.N.S. and you have paid the consulate fee of $150, you can travel to the foreign country to bring your child home.

What will our foreign attorney be required to do to complete our adoption?

The attorney will follow the adoption laws of that country to legally complete your adoption. There are four general steps the attorney must complete for you:

1. Obtain the child's birth certificate, which will provide proof of the child's identity.
2. Obtain a written notice of relinquishment stating that the birthparent relinquishes all claims to the child. This can also include a certificate of abandonment from an orphanage or, in the case of death, the biological parent's death certificate.
3. Obtain a notarized statement signed by the birthparents,

indicating that they agree to the adoption of the child by you. (This is not required by all countries.)

4. Attend the actual adoption proceedings before the judge on your behalf. Some countries require that one or both parents see the child prior to adoption. In other countries you are required to travel only to pick up the child or the child may be brought to the adoptive parents by an escort.

Our best friends had an adoption fall through at the last minute here in the U.S. Is this more or less likely to happen in a foreign country?

It is less likely for an adoption to fall through in a foreign country. In other countries birthparents do have the right to change their minds about the adoption before the actual issuance of the adoption decree. Some countries will not allow the birthparent to sign the relinquishment papers until you have arrived in the country. The final decree comes more quickly in most foreign countries than it does in the U.S., where states generally have a waiting period of six months to a year before issuing the final adoption decree. In many countries you will receive the final decree on the day of the court adoption proceedings. There may be a waiting period of up to three weeks, during which the birthmother has the chance to change her mind. In countries where this waiting period is in place, you can petition the judge to waive this requirement.

Should we be afraid that the birthparents may try to locate us and sometime in the future attempt to take back their child?

When you leave to return home with your child, the adoption will have been completed in that country. Remember that the child you adopt will in most cases have come from extreme poverty. There is virtually no chance that the birth-parents would have the means to travel to the U.S., and if they did there is no recourse here for them to take back the child. Adoptive parents of foreign-born children will tell you that there is an added feeling of security after they return to the U.S., knowing that the adoption will never be challenged.

Here is a suggestion: If you choose to keep in touch with the birthfamily and are concerned that they may try to come find you, provide them with an address (to maintain contact) of a friend or family member in another state, or your agency's address. Some families send pictures and letters without including a return address. To most birth families, the United States is a strange and unknown land. They often will not understand or know where your state is, let alone the town or street you live in.

Travel Considerations

I hate to fly. Are adoptive parents always required to travel to the foreign country to bring their child home?
Many countries require that at least one adoptive parent travel to obtain the child. Sometimes both parents must travel to complete the adoption. Some countries will allow the child to be brought to the U.S. by an escort. Your agency will tell you what is required. If you do not want to travel, let your agency know this up front. They can help you choose a country that will meet your needs. We highly recommend that you travel to the foreign country to pick up your child. Doing so will give you a better understanding of your adopted child's heritage, culture, and background. Years later your child will relish the stories and pictures of your travel to his or her birth country.

We have never traveled outside the United States before. How do we go about making travel arrangements?

Your agency will help you make all your travel and lodging arrangements, beginning from the time you leave until you return home. The agency should provide you with a full travel itinerary. They will also assist you in preparing for the trip, informing you about items to pack, any immunizations that are required, medications to have on hand, gift items, supplies that the orphanage may need, other baby and child supplies, as well as information concerning local customs and culture (what to do and what not to do).

If you have friends or contacts in the foreign country, or if you work for an airline, you may be able to reduce your travel and lodging costs. Also, ask your social worker how to reduce these costs.

Will it be cheaper for us to choose a country in which to adopt that will allow us to use an escort?

Using an escort can save some money. You will not see substantial savings, though, because you must pay for the escort's airfare, the child's airfare, and escort services (several hundred dollars). Escort services will save you time, however, from traveling to and from a foreign country.

We are looking forward to traveling to pick up our child, but we don't have passports. How can we get them?

You both will be required to have a passport to travel to a foreign country. Go to your local post office and ask for a passport application. (Some cities have only one post office that handles passport applications.) You can fill out the application at the post office and give the postmaster the required fee and your proof of citizenship (such as a birth certificate). The postmaster then mails the application for you, or you can mail it yourself. You will receive your passport within two to three weeks. If you need to travel before the two to three weeks, state your departure date and you will receive your passport sooner. Your adopted child will also need a passport to travel to the U.S. You can easily get this in the child's birth country.

Children from Orphanages

We know that many children available for adoption abroad have spent the majority of their lives in orphanages. What kinds of problems should we expect?
You can expect a variety of adjustment difficulties from children who have spent the majority of their lives in orphanages. These children have never been alone. Orphanage children share beds, the few toys available, clothes, and the attention of a few caregivers. Expect to experience some of the following problems with your newly adopted child:

- **Withdrawal and shyness.** Your child may be fearful and overwhelmed by the sudden changes in his or her life. In institutional care the child was taught that passive behavior is good behavior. The child may be afraid that you will suddenly disappear just as the workers and friends he or she has always known. You will need to let this child be introduced to his new life gradually.
- **Clinging to one family member.** Your child will be overwhelmed with the new environment and may try to simplify things by becoming attached to one person. Your child may cling to the parent who traveled to get him or her. The child may become attached to a sibling. Be patient. Give your child lots of love, and slowly show the child that you are a whole family. If you will not rush

or scold your child for clinging behavior, you will find in time that he or she will grow to love and accept all members of the family.

- **Sleep problems.** Your child may experience nightmares or a fear of going to sleep, or may refuse to sleep alone. This is the time to consider your child's cultural background. If, for example, your child is from Korea, he or she would have slept on a mattress on the floor in the orphanage. Remember your child has probably experienced abuse that you have not been told about. Think about how difficult it is for you to sleep in a strange bed when you travel. Let your child sleep in your room at first, and gradually let the child become accustomed to his or her own bed.

- **Toilet habits.** Do not be surprised if your older child begins to wet the bed and/or experiences diarrhea and stomach upsets. As soon as you have your child at home, take him or her to be examined by your pediatrician. Your child may be experiencing upsets because of the change in food and water, but could also be harboring parasites. It is a good idea to have your pediatrician check a stool sample every four weeks for six months, since some parasites are long incubating and may not show up for six months.

    Your toilet-trained child may experience bed-wetting due to underlying stress and a need for control in his or her life. Ask your pediatrician to suggest ways you can help your child overcome the bed-wetting. Most importantly, be patient with your child.

- **Strange eating habits.** Your child will probably refuse new and strange foods. Orphanage children are given a very limited diet. Your child may have subsisted on a diet of rice and beans or soup and bread, depending on the country he or she came from. Many children also tend to hoard or overeat food because they were underfed in their birth countries. Introduce your child slowly to new foods. Find out what foods your child is used to eating, and in the beginning include these foods frequently in his or her diet.

- **Hyperactivity and sudden mood changes.** You may find upon arriving at home that your child begins to throw temper tantrums and seems to be uncontrollable. Remember that your child has come from a very structured environment. Suddenly he or she is experiencing new sights, sounds, and smells, and a completely new level of stimulation. Help your child deal with overwhelming feelings by giving him or her "time out" in a quiet environment. Always stay where your child can see you. Gradually introduce him or her to new stimuli before you make the journey home.

Remember: Patience, consistency, firmness, and above all, lots of love will help your child overcome months and years of institutional care. Your child may require some degree of therapy from a professional counselor in the event the child experiences difficulties in overcoming the above-mentioned problems.

We would like to visit an orphanage and choose our own child. What should we look for?
If you plan to choose the child you will be adopting (as in private adoption), you will need to look at the physical and mental health of the child. Before you travel, get a developmental chart from your pediatrician. This chart will outline what a child at any specific age should be doing. Ask your pediatrician to tell you what to look for in the age range of

the child you want to adopt. Expect children from orphanages to be behind developmentally. Many of these children can be helped to develop to their age level with patience and work. The younger the child, the faster he or she will reach full potential. Look for as healthy a child as possible.

Get on eye level when interacting with the child. Ask yourself these questions:

- Does the child look directly at me?
- Will the child let me touch or hold him or her, or does the child pull away from me?
- Does the child rock uncontrollably, cry, tremble, or seem afraid of human touch?
- How does the child react with his or her environment?
- Are the child's eyes bright and communicative?

Look at and get a copy of all medical records available on the child. Do not be surprised if you find little or no information. Talk to your child's caregivers at the orphanage. They may be able to add some insight about the child.

Independent International Adoptions

We have been touched by reports of abandoned children we have seen on TV. We would like to adopt from an Eastern European country but don't want to work with an agency. Can we adopt independently?
Yes. Independent international adoption can be successful and may require less money and time than an agency adoption. A successful independent international adoption requires that you have a good working understanding of the foreign country's adoption laws and a trusted contact who will guide

you in locating an adoptable child and in going through the adoption process in the foreign country. Since some countries do not allow independent adoptions, it is important to find out which countries do allow them. The trend internationally is to require prospective parents to use an adoption agency that has been approved by the foreign country. Call the State Department or the nearest I.N.S. office and inquire about independent adoptions in the country in which you are interested. The State Department can provide you with your foreign country's adoption laws and a list of requirements. They may also provide you with the names of foreign attorneys and translators.

Whom do we contact in the State Department to receive information on the country we are interested in?
Updated information on foreign adoption is available by recorded message from the Office of Citizens' Consular Services of the U.S. Department of State. The number is (202) 647-3444. You can leave your address and request that a packet of adoption information be sent to you.

What requirements do we need to complete in the U.S. before traveling to adopt overseas?
The requirements are the same as those of an agency:

- Talk with parents who have adopted from your country of choice. You can locate these parents through local and national adoption support groups. We have listed a number of support groups for you in the chapter titled "Adoption Resources." The information and suggestions they can provide for you will prove invaluable.
- Complete a home study provided by a reputable agency or social worker.

- Apply for an I-600A preapproval from Immigrations.
- Complete a dossier to be used in your international adoption. A list of all required documents can be obtained from the state department or the I.N.S. These documents must be certified copies and/or must be notarized.
- Make contact with a reputable source in the foreign country who will assist you in locating a child to adopt and in completing the adoption of the child in the foreign court and who will assist you while you are in the foreign country.
- Apply for a passport and check with the stateside foreign embassy to see if you will be required to obtain an entry visa to the country before you travel. Most countries will allow you to get an entry visa when you arrive at the airport in their country. You can get the number of the foreign embassy by calling information in the Washington, D.C., area. The information number is (202) 555-1212.
- Check with your public health department to see if you will be required to have any immunizations.

In-country Contacts

We would like to travel to adopt soon. If we have been unable to find a good foreign contact, can we go ahead and travel and then find someone to help us adopt when we arrive?
We strongly suggest you do not travel until you have located a contact person and have talked with him or her by phone. Some people have traveled to a foreign country to adopt and have hired the first English-speaking person they met (many times the taxi driver who drove them from the airport). In

some of these cases the adoptive parents have reported completing a successful adoption and making friends for life with their foreign contact. Others were taken in by friendly people who involved them in black-market adoptions in which they were eventually forced to hand over large sums of money to complete their adoption. Do not involve yourself with a black-market adoption. It can be costly and heartbreaking if you are unable to adopt the child you have become attached to.

If you are unable to locate a contact through a local or national support group or through other individuals who have successfully completed an adoption in the country in which you are planning to adopt, try talking to various church denominations. Many church organizations have missionaries who work in foreign countries. You may be able to write to a missionary and get the name of a trusted national who would be willing to work with you.

Will we need to hire an attorney in the foreign country who will finalize our adoption and appear in court with us?
It is very important to follow all the legal adoption guidelines in the foreign country. Some countries require that you use an attorney to complete the adoption. Other countries allow the adoptive parents, or someone with their power of attorney standing in for them, to legally complete the adoption. Successful independent adoption requires that you follow all the rules and regulations of the country. (For example, Brazilian law states that no money can exchange hands for the adoption process, with the exception of attorney fees.) *Note:* The use of an attorney *during* the adoption process is not mandatory in many countries.

Living Arrangements Abroad

We will be making our own living arrangements while we are abroad. We can't afford to stay in an expensive hotel. Do you have any suggestions for finding reasonably priced accommodations?

Ask your contact to locate a family who would be willing to give you room and board. If possible, ask for a family who speaks some English, but don't turn down a family who is unable to speak English. In Third World countries, a family makes an average of thirty American dollars a month or less. You can agree beforehand to pay the family about ten American dollars a night. This will help you keep your overseas cost down and will financially help the family you are staying with. You will have the opportunity to make lasting friendships in the country of your child's origin. If you expect an extended stay, or if you do not want to stay with a family, ask your contact to locate a furnished apartment you can rent. This will be more cost effective than a hotel.

My wife and I have not traveled outside the United States before. Do you have any tips for surviving in a foreign country?

- **Respect the culture.** It is advisable before you travel to read up on the country you will be visiting to learn about the people, food, customs, and history. Talk to people who have visited the country, and ask them for advice and insights. Being aware of cultural differences will prevent you from offending your host. In a foreign country, always expect the unexpected!
- **People of various cultures may react to situations differently from what you are used to.** They may also

be offended by your reactions. Some cultures, for example, feel that laughing in public is inappropriate; they may be offended also by outbursts of anger, or they may consider you rude if you rush them. You may find yourself feeling frustrated. You may intend to hurry out after lunch to finish important papers, only to find that all businesses shut down at noonday for three-hour lunches and naps. No matter how angry or frustrated you become, try to respect your host's culture and habits, or in the end it can cost you more time and money.

- **Take gifts for your contact, your host family, and the other people who help you along the adoption path.** Do not be surprised or dismayed if your contact insists on giving bribes to those involved in your adoption. Many cultures complete transactions through a series of bribes, which they consider to be a normal (and sometimes the only) way of doing business. These gifts are usually simple items such as American cigarettes, bubblegum, cosmetics, perfume, a bottle of aspirin, a bag of coffee beans, sunglasses, and small calculators. Be advised that most foreign countries have laws stating that it is illegal for money to exchange hands during the adoption process.

    Beware: You must walk away from any situation in which money or large-ticket items such as cars or TVs are being demanded in order for you to adopt a certain child. This kind of exchange is illegal, and you do not want yourself or your contact to end up in a foreign jail.

- **The local food will be very different from what you are accustomed to.** You may find that eating bread and sheep cheese for breakfast every day leaves you yearning for a McDonald's Egg McMuffin. Try to graciously accept at least a very small serving, even if it is the strangest-smelling and looking food you have ever been offered.

Your host family will want to feed you the best they have and will be concerned about your eating habits. They will be easily offended if you refuse their food. Take along lots of snacks from home that you can eat in your room if you are unable to handle much of the local fare. Do not be surprised if you find you have lost weight during your travel due to the change in food and stress.

- **Study the language of the country to which you will be traveling.** You will need to know such words as *bathroom*, *drink*, *food*, *sick*, and *help*. Most large bookstores have instructional cassette tapes for the more common languages (Spanish, French, Italian, Portuguese, and so on) for the beginner and the traveler. Ask your local bookstore to order any tapes it does not have in stock. Understanding the language even on a beginner level can cut down on your stress level while you are traveling. Take along a pocket dictionary to help you converse with the local people. Many Americans have been pleased to find someone—a storekeeper, a police officer, or a passerby—who understands at least a few words of English when they find themselves in a desperate situation.

Tips for Traveling Abroad

Besides our clothes, what should we pack when traveling to adopt our child?
Never assume you will be able to find what you need abroad. Items you may be able to buy will not usually be the quality you are accustomed to.

    Toiletries: Soap, toilet paper, toothpaste, toothbrush, dental floss, deodorant, cotton swabs, tampons or any other sanitary needs, disposable razors, shampoo, comb and brush, hair products (it is advisable to have a simple hairstyle for traveling), and disposable wipes for cleaning (those that state they are antibacterial are highly recommended, as there may not be much water available for bathing). Any of the items you do not use or finish using will be gratefully received by your contact or host family. Be careful when wearing makeup, jewelry, and expensive clothes. These items are considered signs of affluence in poor countries and can mark you as a target for crime. Keep your makeup and clothes simple, and do not wear jewelry.

Personal Items: A travel hair dryer that will convert to 220V AC 50 Hz (most countries do not use the same voltage that we use in the U.S.); a small mirror; a pocket knife; a small pair of scissors; a calculator; a camera; extra film (as the film you need may not be readily available); a sewing kit; money pouches to wear around your waist and/or neck (be sure to keep your money and valuables with you at all times); a front pack for carrying small amounts of money, important papers, and your passport; a small heating coil for heating water for tea and soups; snacks; and a flashlight in case you become desperate to find the outhouse in the middle of the night.

Snacks: Peanut butter and crackers, cookies such as fig bars, candy you feel you can't do without (items such as chocolate may be unavailable), gum, packets of soup, powdered drink mixes with sugar, packets of sugar substitute, powdered milk for coffee and for drinking (it is advisable never to drink the milk, since it is usually not pasteurized and can contain harmful bacteria), coffee and tea bags (coffee beans will also make welcomed gifts), and a few small cans of meat or tuna for emergencies. Coke and other carbonated drinks may not be available.

Foods for your child: Remember that your child

initially will not be accustomed to American foods. Gradually introduce your child to new foods. Give your child a powdered soy-based formula to cut down on stomach upsets caused by a change in formula. (Formula can be placed in doubled zip-lock bags for easy carrying.) Also take baby cereal, baby food, and snacks for the toddler or older child.

Medical and Travel Supplies

Medical supplies for you and your child: A thermometer (both adult and child sizes), Tylenol (liquid for your child and tablets for you), cough medicine, antihistamines, and decongestants. If you have problems with allergies, talk with your doctor about getting a prescription before you go. Pollution and a lack of cleanliness in the country in which you are traveling can be a problem for allergy sufferers or persons with respiratory problems. You will also need to pack antacids, laxatives, Kaopectate or Imodium AD for stomach upsets and diarrhea, antibiotics for yourself, antibiotics for your child including antibiotic eye and ear drops, vitamins, Nix shampoo or lotion to rid your child of head lice, triple antibiotic ointment, Band-Aids, hydrocortisone cream, Pedialyte powder to rehydrate your child in case of diarrhea (you will have to ask your pharmacist to special order this as it is not readily available), prescription medicine for scabies for your child, and disposable syringes for any blood tests that may be done on your child.

Baby supplies: Disposable diapers; baby powder and lotion; Q-Tips; pacifiers; baby bottles (plastic bottles with disposable liners are highly recommended, as you may not be able to sterilize your baby's bottles); various sizes of baby and children's clothes, underwear, and shoes; an umbrella stroller (invaluable for traveling home and going through customs); a front pack for a small infant; a tape player for playing music from the child's country; simple puzzles, coloring books, and crayons for the older child; a special soft blanket or toy that is given to the child before he or she leaves the orphanage or hospital and that the child can call his or her own. *Warning:* Do not give laxatives or antidiarrheal medication to infants or children without the advice of a physician.

Why will we need so many supplies? What will we do with any unused items we have?

Although this seems to be a lot of supplies, it is important to remember that many of the items cannot be readily located when you are traveling abroad. This is especially true of many of the poorer countries. It is better to have too many supplies than too few. Any unused item will be gratefully accepted by the director of your child's orphanage or by the host person who has assisted you with your adoption. Poverty is a way of life for most of these people; you will be surprised at how well your extra items will be received. *Note:* Check with your airline for acceptable suitcase size and weight limits. Some airlines allow additional luggage without charge if they know that the items are supplies for an orphanage.

Health Considerations

We have heard that many people get sick from the food and water while traveling in a foreign country. Is it inevitable that we will get sick? What precautions should we take to prevent illness?

Talk with your regular physician before you travel abroad. Many physicians will prescribe an antibiotic, such as Bactrium 500, to be taken once a day. Usually you will be instructed to take the medication before you leave the U.S. and to continue taking it while you are abroad. Studies indicate that this may greatly reduce stomach and digestion problems associated with international travel.

To help prevent illness while traveling, do not eat or drink the following items:

- **Milk.** In many countries milk comes directly from the cow to the table without pasteurization.
- **Fresh fruits** that cannot be peeled.
- **Salads and raw vegetables** that you did not prepare yourself and that you cannot peel.
- **Water from the tap.** The bacteria level in water in foreign countries is not monitored and the water is not chlorinated as it is in the U.S. Be careful when brushing your teeth. Do not swallow even a small amount of water. Buy bottled water when it is available, or boil all water for ten minutes before preparing foods and drinks. Remember that ice cubes can be just as contaminated as tap water.
- **Meat** that is not warm or foods that normally should be refrigerated and have not been. Refrigeration is not widely available in many countries. Harmful bacteria will quickly multiply in foods that have not been stored at the right temperature.

Readoption and Obtaining United States Citizenship

Because we have other children, my husband will be the only one to travel to pick up our adopted child. We have been told that our adopted child will be legally ours when we arrive in the U.S. Why does U.S. Immigrations require that we readopt our child?

U.S. law requires, for the protection of the child, that you readopt a child who has been seen by only one parent prior to the overseas adoption. In case of the divorce or death of the parents, the law helps protect the child in any inheritance disputes that may come up between the adopted child and any biological children or relatives.

What is required to readopt our child? Will it be expensive?
When you have returned to the U.S. with your child, contact a local attorney who has previously completed a readoption. Don't be surprised if you have a difficult time finding one who is knowledgeable about the procedures. Begin by contacting reputable firms that deal with adoption. State laws vary in the requirements for readoption, so be sure you understand up front what your state laws entail. The readoption procedure generally is a short process requiring only a small amount of paperwork that you need to sign, the finalized international adoption papers, and a court hearing. You may or may not have to appear before the court. The shorter the process, the smaller the cost of readoption. The entire procedure should not cost more than $1,000 and can be as little as $450.

We were surprised to hear that our adopted child will not automatically become a U.S. citizen. What do we have to do in order for our child to become a U.S. citizen?
The Immigration regulation states that before a foreign-born child can become a U.S. citizen the child must become a lawful permanent resident of the U.S. The child can become a permanent resident by entering the U.S. with a resident visa (which you will have received from the U.S. Consulate or Embassy and will carry with you when you return to the U.S. with your child). Upon returning to the U.S., you will

receive a Permanent Alien Residence card for your child from I.N.S.

How do we apply for citizenship for our child?

You can file for citizenship for your child in two ways:

- The I.N.S. administrative process is the most cost-effective way. File Form N-643, Application for Certificate of Citizenship in Behalf of an Adopted Child, before the child turns eighteen. The child must be unmarried, must have been adopted before the age of sixteen, and must be a lawful permanent resident of the U.S. You will be required to send the adoption papers and child's birth certificate to I.N.S. along with your application. Within a few months after you have filed the application, you will be asked to travel to the I.N.S. office handling your case. Take originals and copies of all papers pertaining to the adoption—the final adoption decree, the birth certificate, your passport and your child's passport, your child's Permanent Residence card, your marriage certificate, any divorce decrees, any correspondence you have had with I.N.S., and any other papers you think necessary. You may not be asked to show any of these papers, but it is important to have them in case you are required to show them.
- You can also naturalize your child as a U.S. citizen through court proceedings. File with the I.N.S. Form N-402, Application to File Petition for Naturalization in Behalf of Child. There is no waiting period. Form N-402 can be completed as soon as the child is adopted and becomes a lawful permanent resident, as long as the child is unmarried and under the age of eighteen. You will be required to go before a judge, and you will obtain

citizenship for your child by admission from the courts. The cost will be higher because in addition to paying the application fee you will be required also to pay court costs. This is a good procedure for older adopted children, who can take pride in the citizenship ceremony.

For more information about naturalization and citizenship, ask your I.N.S. office for the service publication Form N-17, Naturalization Requirements and General Information.

A Summary of the Steps Required in an International Adoption

International Adoption with an Adoption Agency

1. Contact adoptive parents (through adoption support groups) who have completed international adoptions.
2. Apply to an adoption agency that processes adoptions in the country of your choice.
3. Complete the forms required by the Immigration and Naturalization Service. Pay the required fees.
4. Complete or update your home study with the social worker at your agency.
5. Obtain state approval to adopt if required by your state's adoption laws.
6. Get all the required documents for the adoption translated into the language of the country from which you will adopt your child. This is normally done by your agency.
7. Accept the agency's referral of a child to adopt. International adoption proceedings will then be initiated by the attorney or agency personnel residing in the country of choice.
8. Travel to the child's country. You may attend the court proceedings.

9. Be sure that you receive all the legal documents from the country from which you are adopting. You may be able to take physical possession of your child before the final adoption decree is issued.
10. Obtain the child's medical documents, passport, and visa.
11. Be sure someone from the agency is available to translate all the documents into English, and have the documents notarized. Go to the U.S. Consulate or Embassy for your child's visa appointment.
12. Receive the child's immigration visa and then you are free to travel home. *Do not open the packet you are given.* This is for U.S. Immigrations only.
13. Take your child home.
14. Readopt your child in a U.S. court. Obtain naturalized citizenship for your child.

Independent International Adoption

1. Contact adoptive parents (through adoption support groups) who have completed an international adoption.
2. Contact the U.S. State Department to find out about adoption laws in your country of choice.
3. Establish an independent contact in the country of your choice.
4. Instruct your in-country contact to locate several adoptable children.
5. Complete all the required paperwork for pre-approval from the Immigration and Naturalization Service.
6. Complete the necessary documentation required by the foreign country for your adoption dossier and the home study.
7. Obtain the approval to adopt from your state if required.
8. All of your documentation should be translated and

notarized. You will need five to six notarized copies of each.

9. Send all of the documents to your in-country contact. *Note*: It may prove cost effective to have your documents translated within the foreign country in which you will be adopting.
10. Travel to the country and choose a legally abandoned child to adopt.
11. Locate a resident attorney and initiate the international adoption proceedings. (An attorney may not be legally required. You may be able to file all paperwork with the help of your contact.)
12. Be sure that you receive all the legal documents from the country in which you are adopting at the completion of the adoption. (You will need multiple, notarized copies.)
13. Obtain the child's medical documents, passport, and birth certificate as required by the U.S. Consulate or Embassy.
14. Hire someone to translate all the documents into English, and have the documents notarized.
15. Make an appointment to receive the child's immigration visa from the U.S. Consulate or Embassy. *Do not open this packet.* This is for U.S. Immigrations only.
16. Take your child home.
17. Readopt your child in a U.S. court. Obtain naturalized citizenship for your child.

Chapter 6

SINGLE-PARENT ADOPTION

*T*he desire for a family is a strong and universal need. Married couples are not the only people who want to adopt. Today many single adults face a dilemma. They are financially and emotionally independent, with a strong network of friends and family, yet these adults have not found their life mates. The single adult may feel he or she has much to offer a child. The indefinite wait to find a life partner before parenting a child may be unacceptable to the single adult. As one single mother of an adopted child stated, "I felt I was losing my best child-rearing years waiting for Mr. Right. I wanted a child and knew I'd make a good parent. Adoption was the answer for me."

Although the two-parent home consisting of a mother and a father continues to be viewed as the ideal situation for child rearing, single-parent homes are becoming more widely accepted in the U.S. This is due in part to the soaring divorce rates and to our society's push for extensive male involvement in child rearing.

This does not mean that singles find adoption an easy proposition. Agencies remain reluctant to place infants and small children in single-parent homes. Singles are often offered a chance to parent only the hard-to-place children that an agency has in its care. Parenting these special children can prove very rewarding, although it can be difficult for a single parent to raise a child with medical problems or handicaps requiring constant supervision and attention. Single people are finding international adoption to be a viable way to parent healthy infants or young children.

Adopting as a single adult may be difficult, but it is not impossible. Single people desiring to adopt will find their motivations for adopting, as well as their personal lives, closely scrutinized. A single woman may be asked to explain why she would adopt when she could simply become pregnant. This is a personal decision, yet it is a question many women have been asked during their initial interviews with adoption agencies or counselors. Single people seeking to adopt face issues similar to those encountered by couples who are adopting special-needs or foreign children. We suggest you read the chapters on foreign and special-needs adoptions for additional information. A child may be waiting just for you. Remember, single people can successfully adopt.

I am a single female who is considering adoption. I own my home and have a good income. Is it legal for a single adult to adopt a child?
Yes, it is legal in every U.S. state and in Canada for a single adult to adopt.

Information about Single Adoption

Where can I get information for singles interested in adoption?
Write and ask for:

> The Handbook For Single Adoptive Parents
> Committee for Single Adoptive Parents
> P.O. Box 15084
> Chevy Chase, MD 20825

Where can I find support groups who work with singles?
Contact the following:

> Single Parents With Adopted Kids (S. W. A. K.)
> 4116 Washington Road, #202
> Kenosha, WI 53144

> The National Adoption Center
> 1218 Chestnut Street
> Philadelphia, PA 19107
> 1-800-TO-ADOPT

See the chapter titled "Adoption Resources" for additional information on support groups for singles.

Personal Considerations

I am a thirty-seven-year-old single person. I am afraid that I may not be allowed to adopt because of my age. Are there any age requirements for singles who want to adopt?
Most agencies, public and private, require a prospective single parent to be at least twenty-five years old. The cutoff

age varies between agencies with forty being the average. Some foreign countries require a parent-child age difference of no less than eighteen years. This means that a twenty-five-year-old man or woman would not be allowed to adopt a child more than seven years old. You may be able to adopt until you are forty-five or fifty years old.

I am a single person considering agency adoption. What questions will I be asked during the initial interview?
Specific questions will vary from agency to agency. However, you may be asked a few of the following questions:

- Why do you want to adopt a child?
- What kind of child do you envision yourself parenting?
- How important is the age of the child? Do you want an infant or young child? Would you consider adopting a child nine years old or older?
- Do you want a child of the same race as you, or would you consider a child who is biracial or a child from a foreign country?
- How will you manage the financial responsibilities you will encounter as your child's sole means of support? Can you adequately provide the finances to cover the cost of day care, medical care, schooling, and extracurricular activities?
- Who will care for your child while you work?
- Who will have custody of the child in the event of your untimely death? Will monies be provided to the guardian to cover your child's living and long-term education expenses?
- Are you able and willing to provide a home for a hard-to-place child with special needs or learning disabilities?

- If you are willing to parent an older child, how will you prepare yourself to handle the problems that many of these children exhibit as a result of past abuse (physical, mental, or sexual)?
- Do you have an adequate support system to help you through difficult times—friends or family who would help you during financial difficulties and who will provide you with emotional support?
- Have you considered the impact that a child will have on your social life? How do you intend to handle dating and intimate relationships when there is a child in your life?

These questions are not meant to discourage you from adoption. They are intended to help you decide what you want and expect out of life and to help you better understand the lifetime commitment that it takes to raise a child. Having carefully thought through these questions, you will be better prepared to face what lies ahead.

Choosing a Child

I have heard that single people are only allowed to adopt handicapped children. Is this true?
Single adults seeking to adopt cannot be prohibited by law from adopting any available child. However, the most frequent complaint of single adults seeking to adopt is that most adoption agencies, private and public, place all healthy infants in two-parent homes. This policy has led many single adults to choose international adoption.

Public and private adoption agencies are usually eager to find loving and supportive homes for children with special needs. They will often lower or eliminate the standard placement fees to help make the adoption of a special-needs child financially feasible.

How does a child become classified as a special-needs child?
A child is classified as a special-needs placement if he or she is part of a sibling group of three or more; is school age; has mental, physical, or emotional disabilities; is biracial; or is a child from an ethnic minority. If you feel you would like to parent this kind of child, you will find that many adoption agencies are happy to work with you.

Single Men

I have heard that it is more difficult for a single man to adopt than it is for a single woman. Is this true?
While many single men have successfully adopted children, a man may face more opposition than a woman. Some foreign countries will not allow single men to adopt.

Why is it more difficult for single men to adopt?
Unfortunately, today's society persists with the outdated belief that men are incapable of the sensitivity and nurturing qualities necessary to raise a child. Men also find their motives for wanting to adopt seriously questioned. However inaccurate this notion may be, unmarried men over thirty are commonly suspected to be homosexuals by adoption agencies, social workers, and adoption counselors. To complicate matters, another misconception includes the belief that older or homosexual men are child molesters. When people wrongly put these two ideas together, they end up believing that single men over thirty are homosexual men who adopt young boys in order to abuse them. Ever-increasing divorce rates create thousands of single fathers a year. Many

of these men take active roles in the raising of their children. These fathers are working to enlighten and inform people, changing their beliefs through education and legislation.

I am a thirty-nine-year-old single man. How can I improve my chances of adoption?

A personality test is a good way to begin convincing agency personnel that you are a good potential parent. Ask the agency personnel to recommend someone who can administer a psychological evaluation or a personality test. The Minnesota Multiphasic Personal Inventory is one popular personality test.

How important is a personality test or psychological evaluation?

It can be very important. A person who is sexually attracted to children can be identified through psychological evaluations. Your willingness to take these tests will help prove to the agency that your concern for these children is genuine and that you will make a good parent.

Are there any children who are more suited for adoption by single men?

Yes. It has been proven especially beneficial to place boys needing strong male role models, firm discipline, and guidance with single fathers. It is believed that these fathers can better provide the environment needed for raising emotionally disturbed boys with acceptance and love.

Advantages of Single Adoption

I realize there are several disadvantages to single parenting. What are some of the advantages?

The opportunity to share a family relationship is the benefit that most single people consider when they think of adoption. Today many agencies find that single-parent placements can be ideal for parent and child. Single-parent placements typically allow the parent to spend a great deal of time responding to the needs of the child, while building a strong and solid parent-child relationship. The child can form a bond with this parent. It may be the child's first experience with a stable relationship. This setting gives the child an opportunity to recognize and attain his or her fullest potential.

Which children benefit most from single-parent homes?
Studies have shown that children who have been subjected to complex relationships, those who have suffered physical or sexual abuse, and those who have had numerous foster home placements do extremely well in the simplified environment of a single-parent home.

International Adoption

I am single and am considering an international adoption. Can you tell me which countries currently accept applications to adopt from single women?
Political upheaval and civil disruptions affect foreign adoption policies. Check with the U.S. Immigration and Naturalization Services (I.N.S.) before you begin any adoption proceedings. At the time of this writing, Brazil, El Salvador, Honduras, Peru, Bolivia, and Eastern European countries such as Romania, Albania, Bulgaria, and the Russian Republic accept adoption applications from single women.

Where to Begin

I am a single thirty-three-year-old woman considering adoption. What should I do first?

Begin by contacting adoption support groups in your area. You may be able to locate an adoption support group for singles. Gather as much information as possible on adoption— particularly single-parent adoption. You will meet a wide variety of people in various stages of the adoption process through adoption support groups.

Private Adoption

I would like to adopt privately. I am thirty-five years old and have a secure income. What are my chances?

A financially secure single man or woman may encounter resistance when seeking to adopt privately. Often a birthmother will place her infant for adoption in a home with both a mother and a father, but singles have adopted privately with success. Refer to the chapter titled "Private Adoptions" for hints on increasing your success.

Financial Considerations

A close friend of mine paid a great deal of money to an agency for application and processing fees. She then discovered that this agency rarely placed children with single adults. How can I avoid the same trap?

A few adoption agencies will accept an initial adoption application and its fee from a single person seeking to adopt. The agency may repeatedly prolong and delay the adoption process while continuing to request fees from the prospective adoptive parent. A single adult may use up all available funds or become discouraged and voluntarily stop the adoption process. This practice is not common and is not illegal; however, it is ethically questionable. Ask agencies how many children they have placed with single adoptive parents, and of those placements how many included the placement of healthy infants. Try to determine how long other single adoptive parents had to wait before a child was placed in their home.

Ask the agency to refer you to former single clients who have adopted successfully. Ask these parents how pleased they were with their adoption experiences. Talk to as many adoptive parents as possible. Find out how they were treated by agency personnel, how much time the agency took to place a child in their home, and approximately how much their adoption cost.

If you find more than one adoptive parent who was justifiably dissatisfied or concerned, you may want to seriously consider seeking another agency.

My financial adviser recommends that I have an adoption budget. What is an adoption budget?

An adoption budget is the amount of money set aside to cover the expenses incurred by an adoption. The cost of an adoption can become expensive, especially for people seeking to adopt internationally. A single person who wants to adopt should carefully plan an adoption budget.

Why is an adoption budget important?

Planning an adoption budget before you begin the adoption process can help you determine whether or not adoption is a feasible undertaking for you. Review your overall financial picture to determine your assets and liabilities. This will help you get a realistic idea of the money you have available for adoption.

What are assets and liabilities?
The term *asset* refers to what you own. The term *liability* (debt) is what you owe.

Does a person have to be wealthy to adopt?
No, a person does not need to be financially wealthy or even debt free to afford the cost of adoption. Your financial picture should indicate your ability to budget and to properly manage your finances.

I do not have enough cash to cover adoption expenses. What can I do?
If you do not have the cash needed to cover adoption expenses, there are options. You can liquidate your assets by selling something of value to raise cash. You can borrow against your assets by taking out a home equity loan or by borrowing against the cash values of life insurance policies. Many companies today offer adoption assistance and reimbursements to their employees. If you are working with a limited budget, many financial assistance programs are provided by state and federal governments to encourage the adoption of special-needs children.

What should I include in my adoption budget?
Investigate adoption expenses in your area. Determine the approximate cost of the various avenues of adoption available to you (private, agency, state, and international). Then decide which is the most cost-effective avenue for you.

In planning your adoption budget, you should consider:

- The actual cost of the type of adoption you are considering—Do you have money readily available as needed? What can you afford to pay?

- Increased cost to you of raising a child—Will you need a larger home? Will you need to buy additional furniture?
- Cost of additional insurance—including medical insurance.

What kinds of fees should I expect to pay an agency?
Agencies should tell you up-front what your adoption will cost. The adoption fee should cover all expenses of the adoption. This fee is usually paid in installments, and includes the application, home study, birthmother expenses, attorney, and court fees. Agency fees are between five thousand and twenty-five thousand dollars.

Why is there such a broad range in agency adoption costs?
Many adoption agencies use a sliding scale to determine the cost of an adoption. These fees are based on a percentage of your annual income—usually between 5 and 25 percent. The sliding scale system allows everyone the opportunity to adopt.

What expenses should I expect to pay if I choose private adoption?
All expenses in a private adoption are separate and can be paid as you go. This is one advantage of private adoption. You will be responsible for the cost of a home study, the cost of medical care for the birthmother and newborn, attorney fees, and court costs. See the chapter titled "Private Adoption" for more information.

Does the IRS offer any tax breaks to adoptive parents?
Yes, the IRS does offer tax credit for children. The tax credit that most people are familiar with entitles a tax exemption for each dependent. An adoptive parent can claim this exemption prior to the completion of an adoption if it can be proved that more than half of the child's support

was provided by the adoptive parent. This credit is possible only if no one else claims the child as a dependent. In addition there is a tax credit for single parents called Head of Household tax deduction. You can deduct up to 10 percent if your gross annual income is less than twenty-five thousand dollars.

Another tax credit offered by the IRS is called Earned Income Credit. It is available to taxpayers whose total income is less than $23,240.

Does the IRS offer tax credit for child-care costs?
Yes. The Child and Dependent Care Credit gives parents who must have child care in order to work a direct credit against their income tax. This tax credit can be applied also to the care that any disabled dependent receives outside the home. Your dependent must spend at least eight hours a day in your home. This credit is especially beneficial to any working, single adoptive parent who has a disabled dependent relative or disabled child living in the home. Tax laws are subject to change yearly. You can call the IRS toll-free at 1-800-829-1040 to speak with tax experts. Contact the IRS or your accountant for answers to specific tax questions.

Health Care Costs

Will my health insurance cover an adopted child?
It is important that you understand the conditions of your health insurance plan before you adopt. Health insurance coverage varies. Most insurance companies will cover an adopted child from the moment that he or she becomes a legal dependent (once the surrender papers are signed). Some policies will not cover a child until the adoption finalization, while others will not cover the medical conditions

of a special-needs child if those conditions are considered preexisting. Investigate your health insurance plan before you begin your adoption plan to prevent any surprises later on.

Child Care

I am investigating child care. What types of child care are available?
Five basic methods of child care are available today: day-care centers, nannies or live-in sitters, after-school programs, live-out caregivers, and take-to caregivers.

What is a live-out caregiver?
A live-out caregiver is a person who comes to your house each day to care for your child. Teenagers and college students typically provide this type of care. Occasionally you may find a retired person who will come to your home to care for your child.

How much does live-out child care cost?
Live-out care averages approximately $125 to $200 a week for full-time care. Some live-out caregivers charge an hourly fee of $1.50 to $2.00, but some charge more.

What is live-in child care? How much does it cost?
Live-in caregivers, sometimes called nannies, live in your home full-time and receive a salary for caring for your child. Live-in care is often provided by non-U.S. citizens or by licensed "nanny" agencies. The average cost of live-in care is approximately $150 to $400 a week. These caregivers are often willing to provide light housekeeping services as well. *Note:* You are considered the employer of the person supply-

ing live-in or live-out care. Legally it is up to you to pay the Social Security taxes and Medicare contributions. If your caregiver wants to receive Social Security and Medicare benefits and can prove that she or he was paid for providing child care to you, you will be responsible for any unpaid back taxes as well as penalties for nonpayment.

What age children do day-care centers and nursery schools accept?

Most day-care centers accept infants. Many nursery schools as well as a few day-care centers prefer children who are toilet trained. This means that the minimum age is between two and three years old (with the maximum age for full-time care at age five). Children can attend day care until they are ready for kindergarten. These centers usually open from 6:00 A.M. to 6:00 P.M. Meals and snacks are provided. Many day-care centers also provide after-school care for elementary school age children with pick-up service at your child's school.

How do I choose a good day-care center for my child?

We recommend contacting a variety of licensed day-care agencies in your area. Find out the age requirements and prices. Next, visit these centers, meet the staff, and view the facility. This will enable you to determine whether the facility is safe and childproof. As you tour each center, ask yourself these questions:

- Is an adequate amount of space allotted for the number of children enrolled?
- Am I allowed to drop by and visit my child unannounced?
- Does the facility include a fenced-in play area for safe outdoor play?

- How is the center staffed? Is the child-teacher ratio adequate?
- What programs and activities does the facility provide? Are the children given "free" playtime as well as structured activities?
- How does the staff handle disruptive behavior in children? How do they discipline the children?
- What meals and/or snacks are provided? Do they meet nutritional requirements?
- Are rest periods for the children scheduled into each day?
- If this center accepts infants, does it have adequate diaper-changing facilities?
- Do the staff members wash their hands before and after diaper changes? Do they properly dispose of diapers and waste?

The answers to these questions will help you decide which day-care center is best for you and your child.

What is a take-to caregiver?

A take-to caregiver is a person who provides child care in her home. She may or may not be licensed by the state to provide child care. A license to operate is not mandatory in most states. Often these women have children of their own, and baby-sitting allows them to stay at home with their children while they earn extra income. You are not responsible for the take-to caregiver's medicare and Social Security contributions.

What are after-school programs?

After-school programs allow children to play and have fun while being supervised by adults. Schools often sponsor these programs and pay their teachers extra money to supervise these children. After-school programs can also be organized by parents, who hire adult counselors to supervise and guide children in a variety of activities such as computer workshops, crafts, games and/or sports. Many day-care centers also provide these after-school services. The counselors (or teachers) may also help some children with their homework. After-school programs are available in schools across the country. Contact your local school-district office or your local YMCA for more information.

Chapter 7

STATE AND SPECIAL-NEEDS ADOPTION

Thousands of children across America are living their lives in the foster care system while awaiting "real" homes. These children are shuffled between foster homes, moving an average of two to six times a year. Many loving foster families have given these children an opportunity to grow and to experience family life, yet these children need more than a temporary home; they need a home to call their own. Although a few special-needs children are adopted through adoption agencies, the majority are adopted through state (public) adoption agencies. Who are these waiting children?

Profile: Jimmy is a bright and affectionate eleven-year-old who is available for adoption. His passions include collecting baseball cards and playing computer games. He will tell you, "I want a real mom and dad, but no one wants a big guy like me. People only want to adopt cute babies 'cause they don't get in trouble at school."

Jimmy is hyperactive and has been diagnosed with attention deficit disorder. His mother placed him in foster care when he was three years old and has had no contact with him since. Prior to treatment, Jimmy experienced violent outbursts, and he has lived in nine foster homes in eight years. Jimmy's doctor has prescribed medication to control the hyperactivity, and Jimmy is responding well. His grades and behavior are improving, but he needs consistency and firm, loving discipline. Currently the state has legal custody of Jimmy.

Profile: Kerrie and Jennifer are sisters, ages five and seven, of African American heritage. Kerrie is extremely shy and is emotionally immature for her age. Jennifer has a difficult time with peer relationships. She is excessively protective of Kerrie and distrustful of all men. When asked what kind of home they would like, both girls say they hope that a nice woman will decide she needs kids and adopt them.

Kerrie and Jennifer are both the victims of sexual abuse. They are seeing a psychologist twice a week. The girls' social worker and their psychologist feel that placement in a stable, nonthreatening environment would be best for the two girls. They are looking for a single woman to adopt both Kerrie and Jennifer.

There are many children available for special-needs adoption. Josh, age fourteen, was diagnosed with cerebral palsy at two months old; Amy is a sweet nine-year-old with Down's syndrome; Michael, age three, was the victim of extreme abuse. The list of adoptable children in foster care seems endless, and adoptive homes are few.

Each year more than a million people in this country consider adoption. Most of these people want healthy, white infants. In this chapter we encourage you to open your minds as well as your hearts to the possibility of adopting a child with special needs.

This chapter will answer general questions about special-needs placements and state adoption. We also cover some of the problems that qualify a child as a special-needs placement, including Down's syndrome, learning disabilities, behavioral problems, and the effects of sexual and physical abuse. We cover some genetically related problems such as autism, cleft lip, cerebral palsy, and muscular dystrophy.

It is our intention to inform you openly and honestly of the ongoing difficulties these children may face.

State Adoption

What is state adoption?
State adoption, or public agency adoption, is an adoption arranged through the Department of Child Welfare Services. The laws governing state adoption vary from state to state. Contact the branch office of the child welfare office in your county for your state's guidelines and requirements.

Who can adopt through the state?
Any U.S. citizen can apply to adopt from the state in which he or she resides. Married couples, cohabiting couples, and single people may adopt, although preference is given to married couples.

We are interested in adopting through our state. Whom will we be working with during the adoption process?
The state will assign a social worker, who will work closely with you.

Available Children

Where do the children available for state adoption come from?

The children who are available for adoption with the state are in the state foster care system. The social worker will involve the foster family in preparing the child to move into an adoptive home.

My husband and I have been struggling with infertility for seven years. Can we apply through our state for a normal, white, healthy newborn?

Very few healthy, white newborns are available through state adoption. States are overwhelmed by adoption applications for these infants and will accept applications only every four to ten years. Once prospective adoptive parents are placed on the waiting list, it can take an additional eight to ten years to adopt a healthy, white infant.

What kinds of children are available through state adoption?

Each child who is available for adoption from your state is generally classified in one or more of the following special-needs categories:

- Handicapped children (those with physical, mental, and/or emotional handicaps)
- Older children (school age and up to the age of eighteen)
- Children of racially mixed heritage
- Sibling groups
- Children who have had previous adoption placement disruptions
- Children of ethnic minority backgrounds

Beginning the Process: Adoption Classes

Can we begin our home study with the state immediately after signing up to adopt?

First, you will be required to fill out an application form and provide the state with information about yourself and the kind of child you are interested in adopting. Next, you will be invited to attend a series of adoption "training" classes. Policies on these classes vary from state to state. In these classes you will learn about your state's procedure for adoption and about the foster care system. You will also learn about the roles, responsibilities, and rewards of foster and adoptive parenting. These classes will provide information on the children available through your state. They will help you to discover your true feelings about special-needs children and to determine whether or not adoption is the right course for you.

We are not interested in becoming foster parents. Why do we have to spend time learning about the foster care system?

Children available through the state have been involved with the foster care system to varying degrees. Many of these children have spent the majority of their short lives with foster families. It is important for you to understand the foster care system if you are to deal successfully with the issues and problems of your adopted child.

What are some of the specific things we will learn?

You will learn about characteristics of the adoptive family, such as the following:

- **Boundaries:** Is your family "closed" or "open"? Will you be able to accept a new family member who brings along a different past, a caseworker, and a birthfamily?

- **Roles:** Each family member has a unique role. How will the addition of a child change your family's role structure?
- **Rules:** Each family develops a set of rules that keeps that family running smoothly. Families have spoken and unspoken rules about their actions, dress, foods, and friends. How will you help the adoptive child adjust to your family's rules? How will you react if your child does not adjust to these rules?
- **Communication:** A family communicates through its roles, power structure, and boundaries. Will you be willing to help your adoptive child feel comfortable in the way that he or she expresses emotions—even if it is not the way your family communicates?

Choosing a Child

Will our social worker help us choose a child who will fit into our family?

The social worker will want to help you and the child make the adoption a success. Through a series of interviews, in which background, personality, and family ties are considered, the social worker will help you decide on the child who will benefit most from adoption by your family. You will be asked to assess your strengths for adoption, the ways you balance stress and support, the kinds of demands the child will place on your family, and the kind of child you are willing to accept.

My husband and I want to adopt a special-needs child. We feel we can handle a physical handicap, but we feel uncertain about taking a child who has been sexually abused. Will we have any control over the kind of background that the child we adopt comes from?

You will be given a list of special needs to consider. This list will contain many distinct handicaps, both physical and emotional, including a great variety of illnesses such as diabetes and epilepsy. It is very important to be honest with yourself and your social worker when deciding which of these special needs you will consider. Discuss your concerns about parenting a child who has experienced sexual abuse. The social worker should consider your feelings when matching you with a child. Discuss any feelings and concerns you have about other problems a child may face. Be honest about conditions that make you feel uncomfortable. The social worker will work with you to find the right child for you.

Permanency

We attended an adoption orientation meeting. The social worker mentioned the word *permanency* several times. What does this term mean?

Permanency is a very important issue when adopting a child from the foster care system. It means the adoptive child needs a stable environment and a home that is intended to last "forever." A family needs to provide continuing care, a permanent commitment, and a clearly defined legal status, which allows family members to share a common future.

Foster Care

We want the child we adopt to feel that he or she will have a "forever" home with us. How will we know what to do for our child when we don't know the child and the child doesn't know us?

Getting to know children who come from foster homes and who have special needs can present some real challenges.

That is why involving the child's foster parents in the adoption process is so important. The foster parents have twenty-four-hour-a-day contact with the child. They can contribute valuable information about the child to the prospective adoptive parents. This information will help you begin to know your child.

What type of information on our prospective adoptive child can we expect to receive from the foster parents?
With the help of the social worker, the foster parents will be able to give you information on the following aspects of the child:

- Physical health
- Intellectual ability
- Emotional health
- Social functioning
- Relationship with the birthfamily

Adopting an Older Child

We want to adopt a school-age child. Is there anything we can do to help the child deal with all the changes in his or her life?
Children of all ages enjoy looking through their baby books. These books give them a sense of their history. Most foster care children do not have such records of their lives, including photos of themselves as they are growing up. Begin working on a "life book" with your child. The life book is a combination of a scrapbook, a diary, and a story of the child's life experiences. The life book will give your child a clearer sense of identity. Let the child create the life book and include events and items that mean something to him or her. Include any

photos the child has. The social worker will be able to provide you with information on the child's history from case records, from the birthfamily, and from the hospital where the child was born. The foster parents will be a valuable source of information.

What should we include in our child's life book?
Include the following:

- **Birth information:** a copy of the birth certificate, the child's weight and length at birth, and a picture of the hospital where the child was born
- **Birth-family information:** names and birth dates of the birthparents, names and birth dates of any siblings, a physical description of birth-family members, and information on the extended family
- **Placement information:** names and locations of foster parents, names and photos of any foster home children whom the child was close to, names and photos of social workers whom the child has been especially close to
- **Medical information:** immunization records; any medical care the child has received, including places and dates of any surgeries; any medical background information the child may need as an adult
- **Religious information:** places of worship the child has attended, baptism or confirmation records, any award papers from Sunday school
- **Additional information:** Any photos of the child at various stages of development, and stories about the child that are obtained from foster parents, social workers, birthparents, and teachers

What can we expect to be the biggest problem an older child coming from a foster family may face?
One of the biggest problems any child must face when moving to an adoptive home is the feeling of loss. This child has experienced many significant losses: the loss of the birth-family, the loss of a number of foster families, and numerous other losses resulting from changes in schools and friends.

What are some things we can do to help our child with feelings of loss?

- Communicate effectively
- Share parenting insights with the foster family and the child welfare agency during the adoption transition
- Help the child develop a positive sense of self and good self-esteem
- Avoid the use of physical punishment in helping the child learn to set appropriate limits for his or her behavior
- Before the child enters your home, assess the child's impact on each member of your family
- Expect to deal with the issue of loss directly—for example, by discussing it with your child

Adoption Exchanges

We have heard there are many children waiting for adoption here in the United States. How do we find out who they are and how to adopt them?
To find out about children waiting for adoptive families in your area and those available nationally, contact an adoption exchange.

What is an adoption exchange?
Adoption exchanges are an excellent way to find waiting children. Many states have their own adoption exchanges.

Public and private agencies in each state will list children for whom they have been unable to find families. Some states mandate by law that adoption agencies register children with the state's adoption exchange if the agency has failed to find a home for the child within a specific amount of time. Exchanges do not have custody of children but act as facilitators in the adoption process. Adoption exchanges provide their services free of charge. Families interested should register with as many adoption exchanges as possible. You can ask your social worker to register you. Exchanges have a photo listing of all their available children, with a brief history of each child and the contact person for that child.

What kinds of children are available through the adoption exchanges?

Children listed with exchanges are considered special-needs children—those who have additional physical and emotional needs. These children have been in the foster care system for some time and have been difficult to place through the agency that is handling their cases. The majority of these children are over the age of six or eight, and many are from ethnic minorities. Be aware these children have been too difficult to place through normal adoption channels.

We would like to look through an exchange book. Where can we locate one?

Adoption agencies and support groups in your area are a good source for locating exchange books. The state social worker should be able to provide you with one. Many groups subscribe to out-of-state listings and are happy to share these with you. Adoption exchanges list several hundred children, and the lists are updated every few weeks.

Are there any national adoption exchanges we can register with?

The *CAP Book* is a national photo-listing service that registers hard-to-place children from across the United States in order to give them broader exposure to prospective adoptive parents. These children must have social workers who are willing to place them across state lines. The *CAP Book* is updated biweekly, and the cost of a yearly subscription is seventy-five dollars. For more information contact the following:

> The CAP Book, Inc.
> 700 Exchange Street
> Rochester, NY 14608
> (716) 232-5110

The National Adoption Center, which provides adoption information and training, also operates the National Adoption Exchange. You can register with this exchange through your social worker, or if you have a completed home study you may register directly with the exchange. The National Adoption Exchange publishes a quarterly newsletter and a family album that lists waiting children. This organization assists several thousand children and families annually. For more information, contact the following:

> The National Adoption Center
> 1218 Chestnut Street
> Philadelphia, PA 19107
> (215) 925-0200

For a listing of other exchanges, see the "Adoption Exchanges" section of the chapter titled "Adoption Resources."

We want to adopt a child of an ethnic minority background. Are the adoption exchanges a fast way to locate and adopt a child of a minority or mixed-race background?

Using an adoption exchange may speed up your adoption process. But be aware that some people report that using an adoption exchange can make the search seem never ending. You may inquire about a child and be told that the child has been placed on hold or that another family is in the process of adopting that child. Some of the children's social workers may be reluctant to place their children out of county or state, or may have placed their children with the exchange only because their state mandates it by law. Should you run into a difficult search, *don't give up!* Persistence will pay off. Inquiring about a number of children at the same time will help speed up the process.

Special-Needs Adoption

I have heard that it is very difficult to adopt a child unless he or she is classified as a special-needs placement. What does the term *special-needs placement* mean?

Special-needs placement is a term used to describe children who are considered unadoptable or difficult to place in permanent homes.

What makes a child hard to place?

A child with a disability, physical or nonphysical, is considered hard to place. Nonphysical handicaps include learning disabilities, emotional and behavioral problems, and a minority racial background.

In 1992 the National Adoption Exchange released these statistics concerning special-needs children: 85 percent of the hard-to-place children were over five years old; 42 percent were over eleven years old. Thirty-three percent were white; in this group 44 percent had some form of learning disability, 33 percent were mentally impaired, 69 percent had emotional and behavioral problems, and 29 percent were physically handicapped. Sixty-seven percent were black children; in this group 31 percent had learning disabilities, 21 percent were mentally impaired, 43 percent had emotional and behavioral problems, and 25 percent were physically handicapped.

How does a child become classified as a special-needs child?
Special-needs children are categorized in one or more of the following ways:

- Children five years old or older
- Sibling groups of three or more in which the children need to be placed in the same family unit
- Biracial children
- Children of minority backgrounds (Black, Hispanic, or Asian)
- Children with physical, mental, or emotional handicaps ranging from mild and correctible to severely debilitating

We were told that a biracial child is considered a special-needs placement. Does this mean that a healthy infant or child may be considered a special-needs placement simply because he or she is biracial?
Yes, this is unfortunate but true. In many parts of the U.S., especially in the southern states, a healthy infant who is half Caucasian and half African American is treated as a special-needs placement.

Are all children of mixed parentage considered biracial and hard to place?

Anytime you are dealing with the incongruities of prejudice, it is never that simple. Whether or not a child is classified as a biracial special-needs placement depends on where the child lives. If a biracial child lives in a region of the country with a history of prejudice against his or her race, that child will be considered a special-needs placement. This is due to the difficulty that an agency may have when trying to place the child in an adoptive home. In certain regions of the country a child who is half Caucasian and half Hispanic is a special-needs placement. In other regions a child who is half Native American and half Caucasian is considered a special-needs child. The child who is half African American and half Caucasian is most frequently considered a special-needs child, while the child who has an Asian parent is not.

Bear in mind that the adoption agencies are not being discriminatory when they classify a biracial child as a special-needs placement. Special-needs adoptions are often performed by adoption agencies at drastically reduced fees, to encourage people to get these children out of foster care and into permanent homes as quickly as possible for the benefit of those children.

I have heard discussions on talk shows about cross-racial adoption. What does *cross-racial* mean?

A cross-racial, or transracial, adoption occurs when someone of one race or nationality adopts a child from another race or nationality. The talk shows you refer to often address the question *Should white couples adopt black children?* Currently there is a great deal of debate about whether or not the child suffers or loses his or her heritage in a cross-racial adoption.

Are cross-racial adoptions legal?

You must check the laws in your state. Some states and agencies strongly discourage cross-racial (transracial) adoptions, and a few states approve this type of adoption only with a judge's decree. Most states do not object to cross-racial adoptions.

What criteria are used to classify a child as developmentally disabled?

A child who is to be classified as developmentally disabled must meet one or more of the following criteria:

- The child must have a disability that is severe and chronic and that is a direct result of a physical or mental impairment—for example, cystic fibrosis or Down's syndrome
- The disability must have occurred before the child is twenty-two years old—for example, muscular dystrophy or cerebral palsy
- The disability must be one that is expected to continue indefinitely—for example, autism, hemophilia, or sickle-cell anemia
- The disability must be one that functionally limits the child's ability to care for herself or himself or to understand and communicate through language—for example, mental impairment, blindness, or deafness

What does it mean when a child is classified as learning disabled?

The child with learning disabilities is a child of normal or above-normal intelligence who is unable to learn in the typical manner. Learning-disabled children often become frustrated with school. They may "act out" disruptively. The majority of learning-disabled children are boys. Learning disabilities can range from mild to severe and can include problems such as dyslexia or attention deficit disorder. The use of systematic remedial instruction can often help a child overcome and learn to cope with learning disability.

Attention Deficit Disorder

What is attention deficit disorder?
Attention deficit disorder, or ADD, refers to a child's inability to concentrate or to pay attention for more than a couple of minutes despite punishment or repeated requests for compliance. Children with ADD often experience problems in remembering instructions and in following directions. This makes learning difficult.

What are the signs and symptoms of ADD?
Children with ADD are unable to organize things, and they are impulsive and restless. They habitually fail to pay attention and are extremely distractable. Some of these children are hyperactive (extremely overactive).

Is ADD a rare disorder?
Attention deficit disorder is one of the most common behavioral disorders seen today. Approximately 5 to 10 percent of school-age children are diagnosed with ADD. Boys are four times more likely to be diagnosed with ADD than are girls.

Do children with ADD have lower IQs?
No. Typically, children with ADD have normal or high intelligence.

What is the treatment for ADD?
Children with ADD often have behavioral problems requir-

ing counseling by a psychologist or psychiatrist. Family counseling is encouraged. The parents can receive instructions on behavior modification techniques that the child can use at home and at school. The child may need some form of special education, including a smaller class size so that teacher-student interaction is increased and the teacher can have disciplinary control. Your physician may prescribe medication to help your child pay attention and to control any hyperactivity. Some examples of these medications are Dexedrine, Ritalin, and Cylert.

How long can a child take medication for ADD?
If your child's condition is carefully supervised by a physician, the medicine may be safely taken into adulthood.

Dyslexia

What is dyslexia?
Dyslexia refers to reading disabilities in children who have normal vision and normal intelligence. These children are unable to interpret written language accurately. For example, they tend to reverse the letter *b* for *d* and words like *was* and *saw*, and at times they try to read from right to left instead of from left to right.

What are the symptoms of dyslexia?
Dyslexia is characterized by a child's inability to recognize words and letters on a printed page, making his or her reading ability below normal.

How common a problem is dyslexia?
Approximately 10 to 15 percent of all school-age children have

some degree of dyslexia. Reading disabilities are more common in boys than in girls.

What is the treatment for dyslexia?
Currently, special education classes and tutoring by reading specialists are the only treatments available to dyslexic children. These kinds of treatment have proven effective.

Emotional Problems

What constitutes emotional problems in a child?
Behaviors that are categorized as emotional disabilities can include any of the following:

- Lying compulsively or without an apparent reason
- Behaving in an excessively manipulative manner
- Distrusting adults to an abnormal extent
- Appearing well adjusted and friendly while withdrawing from the family
- Behaving in an inappropriately seductive or provocative manner to the extent of "acting out" sexually
- Vandalizing or destroying property

Physical Disabilities

What physical disabilities classify a child as a special-needs placement?
A few examples of the physical disabilities of special-needs children are as follows:

AIDS	Cerebral palsy
Autism	Cleft lip or palate
Blindness	Congenital deformities

Deafness	Hepatitis B
Dwarfism	HIV
Epilepsy	Polio
Exposure to cocaine or other drugs	Spina bifida
	Tuberculosis

Child Abuse

What is child abuse?
Any situation in which a child's health and welfare are compromised as a result of physical or mental mistreatment or neglect is classified as child abuse.

What warning signs should we look for that would indicate that our adopted child was abused?
Joan McNamara M.S., S.W., in her article in the March-April 1993 issue of *Ours,* listed the following signs that may indicate childhood abuse:

- High levels of anxiety and a low frustration tolerance
- Difficulty in concentrating; a tendency to daydream or "space out"
- A tendency to assume the role of a victim, in which the child may appear helpless, hopeless, and irresponsible or out of control
- Flashbacks, intrusive memories, and/or fantasies relating to violence, sex, or general abuse
- Phobic behavior
- Difficulty in understanding cause and effect, in making decisions, and in learning from consequences
- Self-destructiveness, accident proneness, or helpless behavior

- Obstinacy, disobedience, and difficulty with authority
- Passivity, overcompliance, or babyish behavior
- Consistent lying or stealing
- A tendency to set fires; cruelty to animals
- Compulsive behaviors, such as eating disorders, drug use, repetitive rituals, or nail biting

How can an adoptive parent help a child heal the emotional scars of physical abuse?

More often than not, children of abuse have been raised in environments in which love or acceptance was based on conditions. These children desperately need love and affection but don't know how to ask for it or even how to accept it when it is given. Let your child know that you love her or him even when the child's actions are not lovable. Encourage your child to participate in positive family and social activities. Show your child how to form honest, caring relationships with others. Help your child explore ways to increase his or her self-esteem and self-worth. Reassure your child that he or she did not "ask for" or deserve the abusive treatment. Do not allow your child to use the past mistreatment as a manipulative tool to excuse any unacceptable behavior. Help the child to understand what it means to be responsible for one's own actions. As a parent you have opportunities to use creative and consistent forms of nonphysical discipline. Your child may require psychological counseling in order to learn positive ways of expressing negative feelings. Some children use drugs or alcohol as coping mechanisms, and may require intensive treatment for these problems.

Sexual Abuse

How can I tell if my child has been sexually abused?

Children who have experienced sexual abuse may or may not

have any physical signs. They do, however, exhibit noticeable behavioral changes.

What physical signs of sexual abuse should a parent look for?

The physical signs of sexual abuse include any of the following:

- Venereal disease
- Rashes or itching of the genital area
- Scratches and bruises—especially around the breasts, wrists, or genital area
- Pregnancy in very young adolescents (nine to thirteen years old)
- Blood or discharge on bedding or clothes

What are some of the behavioral signs that a sexually abused child exhibits?

The behavioral signs that a sexually abused child may exhibit include the following:

- Sexual knowledge that is advanced for the child's age
- Seductive behavior by the child toward adults or peers
- Extremely aggressive behavior toward young children
- Pseudomature behavior (for example, an eight year old dressing and acting like a sixteen year old)
- Regressive behavior (for example, bed-wetting or daytime wetting by a toilet-trained child)
- Excessive masturbation or masturbation in public places as a response to stress
- Poor peer relationships
- Sudden or extreme changes in behavior
- Eating disorders

- A fear of a particular person, place, or thing (for example, a fear of bathrooms as a result of being repeatedly abused in one)
- A detachment from body sensations and feelings
- Vomiting or gagging without organic causes; difficulty in eating or swallowing
- Poor hygiene, or a tendency to wear several layers of clothing unnecessarily
- Sexual themes in conversation and play
- Soiling and intestinal problems

Will a sexually abused preteen or adolescent exhibit signs of abuse that are different from those of a younger child?
Yes, the reactions of these older children are different. Sexually abused teens may mutilate or cause physical harm to themselves. They may become preoccupied with death. Many teens threaten or attempt suicide. Attempted suicide is a cry for help. Treat any suicide threat seriously, and seek immediate help for your child.

Sexually abused teens often begin to abuse drugs and alcohol. Parents who suspect their child of using drugs and alcohol can help the child receive early treatment. Low self-esteem following sexual abuse can cause teens to become promiscuous. Sexually abused teens may set fires (a behavior more common among boys). A previously honest teen may begin stealing and lying after being sexually abused. Teens who fear punishment if the abuse is discovered, or teens who are sexually abused at home, often run away. A sexually abused teen may use isolation as a means to keep others from discovering the horrible secret. The teen may suddenly drop his or her friends or may withdraw from the family. It is common for the victim of sexual abuse to feel responsible and guilty for the abuse.

Is sexual abuse often found in adoptive children coming from the foster care system?
The majority of children are placed in the state foster care system due to a history of sexual, physical, or mental abuse or neglect. In the United States, one out of every four girls and one out of every eight boys will experience some form of sexual abuse before the age of eighteen. Studies show 75 percent of all foster care children have been sexually abused.

We are in the process of adopting a young child who has been sexually abused. What guidelines should we follow as we establish house rules?
The National Adoption Clearing House lists ten guidelines for adoptive and foster families of children who have been sexually abused:

1. Privacy: Teach the children as well as the adults in your family to knock on the door before entering a bedroom or bathroom.
2. There must be *no* sharing of bedrooms or bathrooms between children of the opposite sex after the first grade.
3. Family members must not walk around outside the bedroom in underclothes or pajamas. This may be overstimulating for a sexually abused child.
4. *No* person may touch another person without permission.
5. Teach the child to say no assertively if someone touches her or him in a manner that the child does not want.
6. Sex education in the home can provide an atmosphere of open communication. When discussing parts of the human body, never use slang or off-color words; use the anatomically correct words for the body. Suggestive or obscene language should *not* be permitted.
7. No secrets: There should not be any secret games

permitted—especially between an adult and a child. Tell your child to inform you immediately if an older child or adult suggests such a game.

8. No tickling or wrestling: These activities put the child in an overpowered position. They can also have sexual overtones for a child.

9. A child behaving seductively or aggressively, or one who begins "acting out" sexually, becomes very vulnerable and makes others vulnerable as well. *Do not* allow this child to be alone with any other children, and do not be alone with the child yourself.

10. Teach your children that everyone has feelings, including sexual feelings, but that it is not always appropriate to act on those feelings.

Ritualistic Abuse

I have heard the term *ritualistic abuse* in the news. What is it?
Ken Wooden, the founder of the National Coalition for Children's Justice, defines ritualistic abuse as bizarre, systematic abuse that is mentally, physically, and sexually detrimental to children. The sole purpose of ritualistic abuse is to implant evil.

How common is ritualistic abuse?
The more that has become known about ritualistic abuse, the easier it has become to detect this abuse in children. It is not a common form of abuse even though it is receiving a great deal of media coverage. Psychologists are making more diagnoses of ritualistic abuse than ever before.

Are the behavioral signs of ritualistic abuse different from those of other forms of abuse?

Much of the behavior seen in children who have suffered ritualistic abuse is the same as the behavior seen in sexually abused children. However, there are a few differences. Children of ritualistic abuse have bizarre nightmares. Some of them have a constant fear of harm, or they are extremely fearful of being alone.

Children of ritualistic abuse often engage in sadistic play (the mutilation of dolls and animals). They may even mutilate themselves. Some of these children show a preoccupation with death and dying.

Birth Defects

What causes birth defects?

According to the March of Dimes Birth Defects Foundation, several factors contribute to malformations in children. Environmental influences such as maternal exposure to viruses, drugs, or radiation during the critical fetal development period account for 20 percent of birth defects. Genetic abnormalities (traits that are inherited) account for another 20 percent of malformations. The remaining 60 percent of all birth defects can be attributed to a combination of environmental factors and genetics.

What is a genetic disease?

Genetic diseases are disorders and disabilities that a child has inherited from his or her biological parents. Inherited diseases are not contagious. A genetic abnormality can cause physical deformities, mental retardation, metabolic disorders, or a progressive deterioration of the body such as muscular dystrophy.

How common are birth defects?

According to the March of Dimes, one out of two hundred

live births in America today will result in an infant with some form of birth defect.

Can it be determined before a child is born whether he or she will have birth defects?
Genetic abnormalities as well as the sex of a child can be determined through amniocentesis, a procedure by which a small sampling of amniotic fluid is obtained. Amniocentesis is not without risk to the mother and the fetus; there is a possibility of spontaneous miscarriage.

Down's Syndrome

What is Down's syndrome?
Down's syndrome is a genetic abnormality occurring in one out of eight hundred live births. Maternal age (over thirty-five) is a factor in the majority of cases, but heredity can also be a factor. Children with Down's are moderately to severely mentally retarded. Forty percent of these children have congenital heart defects. Nearly all of them have poor immune systems, making them highly susceptible to infections. The average life expectancy is approximately fifty years.

Our son has Down's syndrome. He has brought so much love to our family that we would like to consider adopting a child with Down's syndrome. Where can we turn to find information on adopting one of these children?
There is a group that deals solely with the placement of children with Down's in adoptive families. They will be happy to give you information about Down's syndrome and the children waiting for adoption. Contact the following:

National Down's Syndrome Congress
1800 Dempster Street
Park Ridge, IL 60068
(708) 823-7550

I have heard that many children with Down's syndrome have heart problems. Are these problems life threatening, and can they be treated?
Forty percent of the children with Down's syndrome have some type of congenital heart defect. Not all of these heart defects are life threatening. The most common—endocardial cushion defects—usually requires surgical intervention when the child is between five and eight years of age.

What are some of the medical considerations we should expect with a Down's child?
Children with Down's are more susceptible to upper respiratory infections and ear infections. Antibiotic treatment is usually necessary. Also, it is recommended that children with congenital heart defects be given antibiotics when they undergo any dental procedures or invasive medical treatment. The antibiotics are a preventive measure against a serious infection.

What are the developmental considerations for a child with Down's syndrome?
Children with Down's develop more slowly physically and mentally. Exercises to stimulate muscle coordination and muscle strength can be a fun interactive playtime for the child and parent. Music therapy is highly recommended for these children at any age and can be provided by mobiles, music boxes, tapes, and rattles. Parents should talk and sing to their child during individual playtimes. This allows the child an opportunity to recognize and distinguish voices and people.

Allow your child to interact and play with children who do not have Down's. Children learn from imitating and mimicking the actions of others, especially those of other children. Positive interactions can help your child develop valuable learning and social skills. Repetition is the key to learning, and children learn best by repeating pleasurable activities over and over.

Is financial help available for the special education that a Down's child requires?
In November 1979 the Education for All Handicapped Children Act (Pl 94-142) was signed into law. This law applies to all handicapped children three to twenty-one years old and provides special education and related services at no cost to the parent or guardian. Contact your local school system or the Department of Human Services for your county.

What services are now provided as a result of this law?
Special education refers to classroom instruction, physical education, home instruction, and instruction in hospitals and institutions. Basically it is any formal instruction designed to meet the needs of the handicapped child. *Related services* refers to speech and language therapy, transportation, physical and occupational therapy, psychological or counseling services, and diagnostic and corrective services that a handicapped child may require in order to benefit from special education.

A Summary of the Steps Required in a State (Public Agency) Adoption

1. Contact the Department of Child Welfare Services in your county. Request information on children available for adoption.

2. Request a list of requirements for adoption through a state agency.
3. Determine the kind of child you feel you will best be able to parent—for example, a biracial child, a sibling group, an older child, or a child with mental or physical challenges.
4. Apply to adopt.
5. Attend an adoption orientation meeting, if one is offered.
6. Attend all the state-required training classes for foster/adoptive parents.
7. Complete a home study with your designated social worker.
8. Accept assignment of a child.
9. Visit with the child you will be adopting, if visits are allowed.
10. Obtain medical insurance for your child prior to the adoption.
11. Arrange for any counseling your child may need following placement in your home. Your social worker can help you with this.
12. Petition the courts to adopt your chosen child. (Most states provide an attorney for the adoption proceedings.)
13. Apply for special financial support that your child may require to cover existing medical conditions.
14. Before the child is placed in your home, talk with the child's foster parents to get further insight into the care and nurturing your child may need.
15. Take your child home.
16. Legally finalize your adoption through the courts.

Chapter 8

COMMON MEDICAL CONSIDERATIONS

We included this chapter of common medical conditions to aid and inform prospective adoptive parents. It is not our intent to frighten you; we only wish to inform you of possible situations you may face.

Couples adopting privately may find their newborn in the intensive care nursery with complications which occur as a direct result of a birthmother's use of drugs or alcohol. Prospective parents working with an adoption agency will be asked to complete a form indicating medical conditions they can accept in an adoptable child. We have included AIDS, hepatitis A and B, beta strep, fetal alcohol syndrome, conditions in infants associated with maternal drug use, attention deficit disorder, as well as genetic (inherited) illnesses. A brief descriptive explanation of each illness is provided as well as current treatments and ways to manage a child with the discussed disease.

A separate chapter follows, which covers the medical needs an adoptive parent may expect to find in a foreign-born child. Many of these problems are relatively simple to treat.

AIDS

Acquired Immune Deficiency Syndrome, or AIDS, is a collection of illnesses, characterized by the crippling of an important part of the body's immune system. According to the Centers for Disease Control there is overwhelming evidence that AIDS is caused by the human immunodeficiency virus (HIV). The HIV infection is found in the blood, semen, and vaginal secretions of an HIV-infected person.

HIV is transmitted through sexual contact with an infected person or through the shared needles of drug users, or it may be transmitted to an infant born to an HIV-infected mother. Transmission to an infant may occur before, during, or after birth. It is important to note that numerous in-depth studies on the transmission of HIV indicate that the disease cannot be spread through casual contact. There is no evidence of transmission through shared rest rooms, kitchen utensils, razors, toothbrushes, or meals in house-holds with close, daily contact between noninfected persons and HIV-infected persons.

Is every birthmother required to submit to an AIDS screening test prior to the adoptive placement of her infant?
No widespread, mandatory testing of birthparents for the AIDS virus is in effect today. However, many obstetricians and private adoption agencies encourage high-risk birthparents to voluntarily be tested for AIDS. The state-supported

public adoption agencies have individual policies and regulations that determine which high-risk individuals need testing and when the testing should be done.

   Note: The majority of routine perinatal screenings today include testing for the HIV antibody.

How does an agency determine whether a birthmother is at high risk for AIDS?

If one or more of the following ten criteria apply to the birthmother, she can be classified as a person who is at high risk for contracting the AIDS virus:

- The mother uses or has used intravenous (IV) drugs in the past nine years
- The mother has had multiple sex partners
- The mother is or has been a prostitute
- The mother's sex partner has had multiple sex partners
- The mother has a bisexual partner
- The mother's sex partner uses IV drugs
- The mother's sex partner has AIDS or has had a positive HIV test
- The mother has received blood transfusions or blood products between 1977 and March 1986
- The mother has a coagulation disorder
- The mother's sex partner has hemophilia or a coagulation disorder

If the birthmother is HIV positive, will the baby definitely get AIDS?

Only 30 to 50 percent of all infants born to HIV-positive mothers will themselves become infected with AIDS.

If our adopted newborn has a positive HIV test result, how soon will he or she become seriously ill?

A positive HIV test result in an infant does not necessarily indicate that the child will develop AIDS and die. AIDS testing in infants under fifteen months old can lead to false positive HIV results. The reason for this is simple: the mother passes antibodies in her system to the infant in her womb. This child's blood, when tested, shows the presence of the AIDS virus. In actuality the antibodies present in the child's blood may belong to the mother and not to the infant. Any child who is truly infected with AIDS will continue to show positive HIV antibody results from subsequent testing.

What is the life expectancy of a child with AIDS?
According to the Centers for Disease Control in Atlanta, Georgia, 75 percent of the children who are HIV-positive will die within two years of the actual diagnosis of AIDS.

How common is the transmission of the AIDS virus from mother to infant?
According to the Centers for Disease Control, there have been 3,887 documented cases of pediatric AIDS infection since June 1981.

Are prospective adoptive parents required to be tested for the AIDS virus before a child may be placed in their home?
Currently, some states have policies regarding the testing of prospective adoptive parents and foster parents. Some states, as well as many agencies, may require the testing of high-risk persons seeking to become adoptive or foster parents. Many private adoption agencies require AIDS testing of all persons age thirteen and older who are living in the adoptive home.

We have heard that a great many Romanian orphans are infected with AIDS. How can we protect ourselves from adopting an AIDS infant?

All foreign-born children, regardless of age or country of origin, are required to submit to AIDS screening before a visa into the U.S. will be issued. No child with a positive HIV test result is given a visa. *Note:* You should request an HIV test to be performed on your child *before* the final adoption hearing.

How accurate are the results of AIDS testing that is administered in a foreign country?

Some prospective adoptive parents have voiced concern about the accuracy of the AIDS testing that is done in foreign countries, especially in Romania. According to the Centers for Disease Control (CDC), one thousand blood samples previously collected and tested in Romania were retested in the CDC. The results were the same, showing that Romania's testing for AIDS is sensitive and accurate.

Note: The actual risk of HIV infection in a Romanian child born later than December 1989 is very low. This is a result of new blood management practices. The standards used to screen blood for infectious diseases are strictly adhered to, and disposable needles and better equipment are used. Routine blood transfusions are no longer given to malnourished and anemic children.

There is always confusion and fear when people are faced with a disease such as AIDS. Rumors and misconceptions concerning the transmission of AIDS continue to surface. The CDC in Atlanta, Georgia, has a national AIDS hotline (1-800-342-2437) which you may call at any time. Someone is always there to answer any questions you have about AIDS, its transmission, and its treatments.

Beta Strep

Beta strep, or group B strep, is a common bacterial infection that can be transmitted to the infant in the womb or during delivery, even though the mother often has no symptoms of the infection.

Each year approximately 2,200 infants die from this infection; others suffer permanent handicaps such as brain damage, mild to severe retardation, blindness, deafness, and/or severe lung damage. The transfer of group B strep to an infant is easily preventable.

How many infants a year are infected with group B strep?
Approximately twelve thousand infants a year are infected with group B strep (GBS).

If GBS does not harm women, how does it affect their babies?
GBS travels from the mother's vagina into the uterus, or it may be passed to the baby in the birth canal. The infant becomes sick when the bacteria invade his or her bloodstream. Life-threatening conditions such as meningitis, pneumonia, and shock can occur.

Note: Occasionally GBS may affect women adversely: It is responsible for fifty thousand infections of pregnant woman each year. The symptoms may include fever after the birth of an infant, uterine inflammation, and infections following cesarean sections.

In what situations is there a high risk for GBS?
It has been shown that the women who carry large amounts of GBS are the ones who are most likely to infect their babies. There are five high-risk situations for a woman with a GBS infection:

- A fever before or during labor
- A history of previous GBS births
- Premature labor
- A premature rupture of membranes
- A prolonged rupture of membranes before the birth of the baby

Can GBS infections be prevented?

Yes. Medical studies indicate that antibiotics injected into a pregnant woman's veins during labor greatly reduce the risk of newborn infection.

Can we wait to have our infant treated with antibiotics after birth?

The earliest possible intervention is always best. Antibiotics given to the birthmother during labor can prevent an illness in the infant.

How can we know if our birthmother is at high risk for GBS?

Although GBS is found in the genital tract of women, it does not cause symptoms of discomfort, and it is not considered a sexually transmitted disease. Your birthmother's obstetrician can screen for GBS by performing a routine culture during the pregnancy. Obtaining a culture is a simple and painless procedure in which a sterile swab is used to obtain cultures from the vagina, rectum, and cervix, or a urine test is used to determine the presence of GBS.

What if our birthmother is not tested for GBS? Are there other ways to determine the likelihood of infection?

If your birthmother meets any of the high-risk criteria, a procedure called the rapid test can be performed during her labor. This test can determine whether she has a large amount of GBS. If she does, antibiotic treatment can be started before the birth.

Note: Many women carry GBS, and not all of their babies become ill. Many physicians, wanting to avoid unnecessary treatment based on positive cultures alone, believe that antibiotic treatment should focus on the high-risk patients.

For additional information about GBS write to or call the Group B Strep Association:

Group B Strep Association
Department RD
P.O. Box 16515
Chapel Hill, NC 27516
(919) 932-5344

Cytomegalovirus

Cytomegalovirus, or CMV, is a viral infection that falls into the herpes simplex 1 and 2 category. CMV is the most frequent cause of congenital birth defects acquired during pregnancy.

The method of transmission is not completely understood. This is not a highly contagious disease, and it may be transmitted through sexual contact, contact with body fluids, breast milk, and blood transfusions.

Because the symptoms of CMV are vague, few cases are diagnosed. A woman with CMV may have symptoms of mononucleosis—a low-grade fever, a sore throat, and swollen glands—and yet a test for mono is negative. She may have symptoms of hepatitis, but the test results for this disease are also negative.

CMV is more prevalent in low socioeconomic groups and in developing countries. Women of childbearing age in India, Africa, and Asia excrete CMV recurrently.

Women with a first time CMV infection who are infected during the first trimester of pregnancy are the ones who are most likely to have infants with congenital deformities. The results of primary infection to a fetus can be hearing loss, mental retardation, and/or vision loss.

Who should be screened for CMV?

Foreign-born children—especially those from Asia, Africa, and India—should be screened for CMV when they are adopted by women of childbearing age.

Why should these children be screened?

The most important reason to screen children adopted from foreign countries or children from low socioeconomic groups is the immune status of the adoptive mother.

According to the Centers for Disease Control, almost 50 percent of women in upper- and middle-income groups are not immune to CMV. If a CMV-excreting child is introduced into such a home, the adoptive mother may experience primary infection. If that adoptive mother becomes pregnant, her biological infant may suffer birth defects as a result of the infection.

What is the best possible defense against a CMV infection?

The best way to prevent CMV transmission is the vigilant practice of good hygiene and hand-washing techniques. Always maintain careful personal hygiene when changing diapers and when handling toys or other objects which may be contaminated with saliva.

If you are a woman of childbearing age, and adopt a child who might carry the antibodies for CMV, you can choose to have yourself screened for CMV antibodies. If the results indicate you have not built up CMV antibodies, you may want to practice some form of birth control. Studies now indicate women who become pregnant six months after exposure or initial infection will not be at risk during any future pregnancies.

Note: If you have a teenage girl living in your home, she should follow the preceding advice for all women of childbearing age, in the event she becomes pregnant.

The main physical effect of CMV on a woman is simple flu- or mono-like symptoms; there is no real danger to the woman herself. CMV poses its greatest threat to the infants of first-time exposed women during the first trimester of pregnancy. This is the point of development when birth defects are most likely to occur.

Hepatitis

Hepatitis is a viral infection of the liver. There are currently five known types of hepatitis viruses. We will discuss the two most commonly found hepatitis viruses, A and B on the following pages.

The symptoms of any hepatitis infection include loss of appetite, dark urine, fatigue, and sometimes fever. Also, an enlarged liver will cause the skin and the whites of the eyes to take on a yellow tinge. Hepatitis may be acute, occurring as a one-time infection, or it can become chronic (repeated infections).

Hepatitis A

Hepatitis A, also known as infectious hepatitis, occurs as a one-time infection. Hepatitis A is transmitted by the ingestion of fecal-contaminated food and water. The person who has had this infection is immune to subsequent infections and will not become a chronic carrier. A person infected with mild hepatitis is treated with bed rest; no drug therapy is used. Children under the age of ten who live in developing countries are more likely to become infected. In developed countries this infection is seen most commonly in young adults.

What treatment will a baby require whose birthmother has hepatitis A?
No treatment is necessary for the newborns of hepatitis A-infected mothers.

I understand that hepatitis A is more common in developing countries and in areas with poor sanitation. How can I protect myself against infection when I travel to Eastern Europe to adopt?
Persons traveling abroad with an intention to stay three months or less may receive an immunoglobulin injection prior to his or her departure. This shot can temporarily boost your natural immune system and ward off many potential infections. During your stay, observe good sanitation and personal hygiene practices, especially hand washing, as an additional preventive measure.

Hepatitis B
Hepatitis B, or HBV, is an infection that may occur in two phases, acute and chronic. The acute hepatitis occurs immediately after the initial infection and may last anywhere from a few weeks to several months. The second phase, or chronic hepatitis, may occur anytime you are infected. Acute hepatitis symptoms may include loss of appetite, fatigue, nausea, vomiting, and stomach pain. Skin rashes and joint pain can occur as well as dark urine and yellowish skin and eyes.
Over half of the people infected with HBV never

exhibit any symptoms of illness. These people, as chronic carriers of the disease, are capable of spreading HBV to others throughout their lifetimes.

How is HBV transmitted?
HBV is found in the blood and bodily secretions of an infected person. It can be passed to another person by contact with bodily secretions—through sexual relations or through the sharing of toothbrushes, razors, or needles used to inject drugs. A baby can get HBV from its mother at birth.

How is HBV treated?
Acute hepatitis B infections receive no specific treatment; care is directed toward the relief of symptoms. Intron A has recently become the first successful treatment of chronic HBV. Intron A, given by injection, is expected to cure approximately 40 percent of those who have hepatitis B.

Can HBV infections be prevented?
Yes. According to the U.S. Department of Health and Human Services, hepatitis B and hepatitis immunoglobulin vaccines will protect 85 to 95 percent of all the people who receive the complete series of three vaccines.

How long will the vaccines protect a person from HBV?
Protection against HBV lasts at least ten years. Currently the U.S. Department of Health does not make any recommendations for booster doses of the vaccine.

If a person can have HBV without symptoms, how can our birthmother determine whether or not she is infected and at risk of passing HBV to her newborn?

Most prenatal screenings routinely include a test for HBV. If it is not included, your birthmother can request a simple blood test to determine whether she is infected. Infants born to infected mothers can be protected from infection by being vaccinated soon after birth.

If our birthmother has HBV, how soon should our newborn be vaccinated?
Pediatricians prefer, whenever possible, to give one dose of hepatitis B immunoglobulin vaccine and the first dose of HBV vaccine during the twelve hours following birth. Subsequent vaccines should be given when the child is one month old and six months old.

Why is it important for infants and children to receive the HBV vaccine?
Nine out of ten infants infected with HBV will become chronic HBV carriers. The younger the child at the time of infection, the more likely that child will become a carrier. Vaccinating infants and children against HBV will protect them once they become teenagers and young adults—the age at which they are most likely to become infected in the U.S.

Who should receive the HBV vaccine?
The HBV vaccine can be safely given to all infants and children. The HBV vaccine is strongly recommended for the following groups of children:

- Immigrant and refugee children under the age of seven
- Infants born to HBV-infected mothers
- Infants less than twelve months old whose primary caregivers have been exposed to acute hepatitis B infection

These children need a dose of hepatitis B immunoglobulin (HBIG) followed by the series of HBV vaccinations.

I have read that hepatitis B is more common in certain countries. Which countries have a high incidence of HBV?
The countries with high incidence of HBV are all of the countries in South America, most of the South Pacific Islands, China, most eastern and southern European countries (including Albania, Bulgaria, Romania, and the Russian Republic), and Middle Eastern countries.

If we adopt a child infected with hepatitis B, how can we prevent infection in other members of our family?
Hepatitis B immunoglobulin (HBIG) is a vaccine that can be given in conjunction with the HBV vaccine. HBIG can prevent infection for one to three months in a person who has been exposed to hepatitis. If you have had contact with hepatitis B infected blood, you must receive the HBIG within twelve to twenty-four hours of blood contact. Good hygiene and proper handwashing techniques help greatly toward preventing the spread of hepatitis B.

What precautions other than vaccination can we take to prevent the transmission of HBV?
- Carefully handle and dispose of all waste materials, including diapers or items contaminated with blood (towels, bandages, Band-Aids, and other first-aid items).
- Use a mixture of one part household bleach to ten parts water to effectively clean blood or saliva from people and objects.
- Do not allow children to share toothbrushes, Popsicles, teething rings, or other objects that can spread saliva.
- Be sure that anyone who is exposed to HBV through a

wound, by mouth or eyes, or through sexual intercourse receives the HBIG vaccine within twenty-four hours of exposure.

Where can a person go to receive the HBV and HBIG vaccines?
All public health departments throughout the U.S. can administer the HBV and HBIG vaccines. Contact the one nearest you for additional information. You may receive the vaccine from your family physician.

Where can we get additional information on hepatitis?
The Centers for Disease Control has a hepatitis hotline: (404) 332-4555.

Tuberculosis

Tuberculosis (TB) is an infectious disease caused by bacteria. Several decades ago, successful treatment of TB with antituberculous drugs virtually wiped out the disease in developed countries such as the U.S. However, a resurgence of the disease has occurred. TB today appears more resistant to conventional medical treatment. The increase in TB cases today is most likely AIDS related. It is more common in areas with crowded living conditions, such as prisons or orphanages.

How is TB spread?
A cough can spread TB. The bacteria causing TB infect a person's lungs, and the droplets of water formed when the person coughs carry this infection to anyone who inhales the droplets. A person can acquire TB also by drinking unpasteurized milk.

What are the symptoms someone with TB may have?

Many people infected with TB do not have any symptoms. Those who have symptoms usually experience fatigue, persistent cough, bloody sputum, fever, night sweats, weight loss, and loss of appetite.

What is the medical treatment for TB?

TB is treated with an extensive therapy of drugs—usually isoniazid, streptomycin, or rifampin. Unlike AIDS, tuberculosis is a curable illness; however, it is usually fatal if left untreated.

How can TB be detected?

A simple TB tine test is adequate for detecting TB in most people. However, The American Academy of Pediatrics recommends the Mantoux intradermal skin test for children living in countries with a high incidence of tuberculosis. The Academy recommends that all children adopted from foreign countries receive the Mantoux intradermal skin test.

The medical records sent with our daughter indicate that she received something called BCG while living in an orphanage in the Russian Republic. What is BCG?

BCG is a live vaccine containing a weak form of TB. The vaccine is used to boost a child's immune status and to prevent the child from becoming infected with TB. It is recommended that only those children who are placed at an unavoidable risk receive the BCG vaccine.

Which children should receive the BCG vaccine?

- Infants and children who live in households with repeated exposure to untreated or ineffectively treated TB patients.

- Infants and children who live in groups with excessive rates of new infections or in groups in which the treatment of TB is not feasible or unsuccessful. Children living in overcrowded institutions and orphanages are prime candidates to receive the BCG vaccine.

If a child receives the BCG vaccine, will it affect TB screening test results?
The BCG vaccine can affect TB test results. A child will have a false positive TB test result for at least twelve months after being vaccinated. A child who has received the BCG vaccine can show a false positive TB skin test result for several years. Consult with your pediatrician to determine whether a child who has received the vaccine should be given any future TB skin test. A reaction at the test site can occur and cause sloughing of the skin. If your physician feels that your child possibly has TB, a chest X-ray will be used for the diagnosis.

Our thirteen-month-old daughter has received the BCG vaccine. When should she be tested for TB?
It is currently recommended that a child who has received the BCG vaccine wait at least one year past the BCG date before the TB skin test is given. This recommendation applies only to children who have no TB-like illness.

If we find our daughter has an active case of TB, what special precautions do we need to take to prevent others in our home from becoming infected?
Children with active tuberculosis are *not* contagious. Any cough that a child may have is usually minimal. Therefore, no isolation is necessary. These children can continue attending day-care while they undergo treatment.

The Premature Infant

A normal pregnancy lasts nine months or forty gestational weeks. A premature baby is one born between twenty-six and thirty-six gestational weeks. Advances in the care of premature infants have increased the rate of survival. Infants as young as twenty-six weeks are now surviving.

The exact cause of prematurity is unknown. Many factors affecting the mother and the baby may be responsible for a premature birth. Certain women, however, are at higher risk for delivering their infants prematurely. They include the following:

- Women who are undernourished and anemic (deficient in iron)
- Women who abuse drugs and/or alcohol
- Women under eighteen years old who have been pregnant more than once
- Women over thirty-five years old who are pregnant for the first time
- Women whose membranes ("bag of water") rupture prematurely
- Women with a history of premature births
- Women who are pregnant with more than one child
- Women who have infections (such as urinary tract infections) which can predispose them to premature delivery
- Women who are experiencing pregnancy-related complications such as bleeding, toxemia, or placental separation
- Women with medical problems such as diabetes, heart disease, or kidney disease

What medical problems can a premature infant develop?
The most common problem associated with prematurity in

the newborn is underdeveloped lungs resulting in the infant's inability to breathe. This is called respiratory distress, or hyaline membrane disease. There is a direct correlation between a child's gestational age and birth weight and the severity of the problems that a premature child will face. The lower the gestational age and weight, the more likely it is that the baby will have developmental or neurological disabilities. Unlike full-term babies, premature babies have few or no natural antibodies to help fight disease. They are highly susceptible to infection.

What is respiratory distress?
Respiratory distress, or hyaline membrane disease, occurs primarily in premature infants. An infant with this disease has an inadequate amount of surfactant (an agent that reduces lung tension). Breathing becomes increasingly difficult for the infant, and finally the infant stops breathing altogether due to exhaustion. When a baby's oxygen is compromised, a tube that is connected to an oxygen source must be placed in the baby's lungs.

What are some of the developmental or nervous-system problems a premature baby may have?
Developmental problems are the problems associated with a child's ability to learn. A child may have a disease such as cerebral palsy, or may have vision and hearing difficulties.

How soon will respiratory distress appear in a baby?
Usually, respiratory distress can be detected within a few minutes of birth.

What are the symptoms of respiratory distress?
A baby who is having difficulty breathing will grunt, and his

or her breathing will be rapid, harsh, and irregular. The baby will also have nasal flaring and a dusky skin color.

How will the doctor decide if our infant has respiratory distress?
The diagnosis of respiratory distress can be confirmed by a blood test showing the levels of oxygen in the blood, by the infant's physical condition, and by X-rays of the chest and lungs.

What will happen to a baby that is born with respiratory distress?
A baby born with respiratory distress will need to stay in a neonatal intensive care unit until his or her lungs are fully developed. Neonatal intensive care nurses will constantly monitor your baby's blood pressure, heart rate, temperature, and respirations. The baby will be placed in an incubator with warm humidified air to regulate the baby's body temperature and to provide the needed oxygen. The baby will receive nutrition intravenously (through the vein).

How long after birth will it take for the baby's lungs to fully develop?
The lungs of a premature baby usually mature within a period of ten days to two weeks.

What are some of the developmental or nervous system problems a premature baby may have?
Many premature infants do not have a gag or sucking reflex; others have extremely small stomachs causing them to vomit frequently. An infant who doesn't have a gag reflex can choke, and formula may be aspirated into the lungs. This aspiration often can cause pneumonia.

Why are some babies fed through tubes?
If an infant is not able to suck properly, he or she will not

receive enough nourishment to grow and survive. A small feeding tube is placed down the infant's throat and into the stomach, allowing the infant to be fed small amounts of specialized formula frequently.

How long will the baby be fed through a tube?
A baby will be fed through a feeding tube until he or she has developed a satisfactory sucking and gag reflex.

Will our baby come home directly from the neonatal intensive care unit?
Once your baby can breathe without assistance, he or she may be transferred to a regular newborn nursery for continued observation. Premature infants can be discharged from the hospital when they can maintain and regulate their body temperature, take a bottle, and weigh approximately 4 to 4½ pounds.

How long must a premature infant stay in the hospital?
The length of stay varies with each infant. It can be a few weeks or several months, depending on your child's condition.

How can we deal with the long separation from our baby?
Most hospitals today strongly encourage parental involvement in the intensive care nursery. Parents are allowed to feed their babies and change their diapers. Parents are encouraged to talk to their babies, touch and hold them. This kind of parental involvement has proven extremely beneficial and has sped the recovery rate of premature infants. Some parents read to their baby, play music in the crib, and paste their picture in the crib. This may seem scary for an adoptive parent. Some may fear that forming a strong attachment to a sick infant is emotionally risky, and it *can* be; yet the benefits can be enormous. The day you finally

bring your child home, you are bringing home your son or daughter, the one you rocked and held and watched struggle for life.

Fetal Alcohol Syndrome

Fetal alcohol syndrome (FAS) is a term that describes a group of disabilities in a child that result directly from maternal alcohol use during pregnancy. One to two infants out of every one thousand live births will exhibit some symptoms of FAS.

Typically, a child with FAS will be a low-birth weight baby and will remain smaller than average. The child may have an unusually small head and some facial abnormalities that include small, narrow, or very round eyes with a shortening of the eyelids. The child may have a flattened midface, a widely spaced nose, a very narrow upper lip, a low-set jaw, and oddly set ears. Congenital heart and kidney defects are common among children with FAS.

FAS children may have ongoing problems such as heart defects, congenital abnormalities, joint and limb difficulties, and mild to moderate mental retardation. As these children grow and develop, behavioral and cognitive problems become evident.

Is there a cure for FAS?

No. Alcohol alters the way a baby develops while in the uterus. These problems can be treated, but the disabilities are permanent.

Is fetal alcohol syndrome more common in foreign countries?

No. Fetal alcohol syndrome as well as other fetal alcohol effects have been observed in children worldwide.

Approximately how many children in the U.S. are born with a full range of FAS symptoms?
In the U.S. today it is believed that approximately 1 out of every 750 newborn infants will have all the symptoms of FAS. This means that approximately 30 to 40 percent of the mothers who drink heavily while pregnant will deliver a FAS child.

How much alcohol can a pregnant woman safely consume and not adversely affect her baby?
No one knows exactly how much alcohol it takes to cause FAS. Current research indicates that women who drink as few as two drinks a week have given birth to children with some of the characteristics of fetal alcohol syndrome.

Maternal Use of Illegal Drugs

Unfortunately people, and particularly pregnant women, are not always open or honest about any drug use or alcohol problems they may have. It is possible that an adoptive couple may be unaware of a birthmother's alcohol or drug use until after her infant is born. The following section deals with some of the more frequently used drugs and their resulting effects on a fetus or newborn infant.

What drugs can an infant be addicted to at birth?
An infant may be born addicted to any substance which easily passes from the birthmother through the placenta into the baby's system. When people talk of drug addiction they usually refer to narcotic drugs (legal or illegal) to which the birthmother is addicted. These drugs can be prescription pain medicine (Demerol, codeine, morphine, tranquilizers, or sleeping pills) or illegal drugs such as amphetamines

(uppers), speed, barbiturates, cocaine, heroin, methadone or phencyclidine (PCP).

Are all babies born to addicted mothers also addicted?
At least half of all the infants born to drug addicted mothers are also addicted and will experience some form of drug withdrawal during the first weeks of life.

Is there a specific drug which is more widely abused than others?
Trends in drug use constantly change. However, cocaine is one of the most widely abused illegal drugs today. The number of cocaine addicted babies seen across the country in nurseries for newborns is on the rise.

What are some of the complications a birthmother addicted to cocaine may experience?
Women who use cocaine or other stimulant drugs are two to six times more likely than a nonuser to deliver a premature infant. These women are at high risk for complications during the delivery, which may result in the need for the baby to be delivered by an emergency cesarean section.

How soon will a drug-addicted infant begin to experience withdrawal?
Most addicted infants begin drug withdrawal within seventy-two hours of delivery. Infants of barbiturate-addicted mothers may not begin drug withdrawal until seven to ten days after birth.

What physical symptoms does a drug-addicted infant experience during withdrawal?
Numerous problems are associated with drug withdrawal.

The infant is irritable and hyperactive and may have a shrill cry. The infant may also experience sleeping and feeding problems. Some babies exhibit an increased respiratory rate, diarrhea, vomiting, or seizures. Other signs of drug withdrawal are a vigorous and ineffective sucking reflex, sweating, excessive tearing of the eyes, sneezing, nasal stuffiness, yawning, and muscle stiffness.

What are some of the complications associated with a drug-addicted infant?

Infants born to drug-addicted mothers are usually premature, making them small for their gestational age. These children have a higher rate of sudden infant death syndrome (SIDS) than do babies born to nonaddicted mothers. Many of these children have behavioral and learning disabilities as they grow.

What is the treatment for a drug-addicted infant?

An infant with a severe addiction may need drug treatment. The smallest drug dose needed to relieve severe symptoms of withdrawal in an infant is given to the infant under close supervision. The drug dosage is slowly weaned away until the infant no longer needs the drug.

How is mild withdrawal in an infant treated?

You can swaddle your infant to ease the irritability and restlessness. It is best to minimize your handling of the infant in the beginning; excessive holding can increase irritability. Keep noises and lights in the baby's environment to a minimum. Your baby is likely to have a poor but frantic sucking reflex; give the baby a pacifier between feedings. It is advisable to feed your baby small, frequent meals. Keep your child clean, warm, and dry.

Is drug withdrawal in infants fatal?
While drug withdrawal is rarely fatal, it can have long-term effects on the health and well-being of the child.

Can infants suffer withdrawal symptoms from anything besides drugs and alcohol?
Yes. Some infants born to women with high caffeine intakes and women who smoke heavily will be irritable, inconsolable, and jittery and may have a shrill cry.

Our birthmother has a history of illegal drug use. Can she be required to submit to routine drug screenings during her prenatal visits?
Neither you nor anyone else can force a birthmother to submit to routine drug screenings. However, if you or your intermediary has established an open and comfortable relationship with your birthmother, you can choose to broach the subject of voluntary drug screenings. Proceed cautiously. It is important for your birthmother to feel you have a genuine concern for her well-being as well as her infant. Do not say or do anything that might make her feel you are passing moral judgment on her. Do not lead her to believe you do not trust her to properly care for herself during her pregnancy. She may become resentful. Simply explain routine drug tests may help you provide medical insurance for the baby after the birth. Bear in mind that if you are unable to present the screenings as something positive that she can do for herself and her baby, she may feel threatened and stop the adoption proceedings.

Sudden Infant Death Syndrome

Sudden infant death syndrome, or SIDS, is the sudden and unexplainable death of an infant who appeared healthy. SIDS is fairly uncommon in children less than two weeks old or more than six months old. It occurs usually between the second and third months of life. In the U.S. SIDS occurs in approximately one out of five hundred live births.

Males are more likely to die from SIDS than females. Other children who are in the high-risk group are premature and low-birth weight infants, infants of birthmothers who smoked or used drugs during pregnancy, and infants with siblings who died of SIDS. Cold weather also has been linked to an increase in the number of reported SIDS cases.

What can we do if our infant is at high risk for SIDS?

Equipment that monitors an infant's respirations can be obtained if your physician deems it beneficial. Some physicians question the reliability of such equipment. If you, the adoptive parents, are given a machine called an apnea monitor, become proficient and knowledgeable in the use of the equipment. We encourage parents to take a pediatric life saving course that includes CPR.

Why is smoking harmful to an unborn baby?

Studies have shown women who smoke one or more packs of cigarettes a day have smaller babies at birth. A smaller baby is weaker and more vulnerable to illness and disease than a normal size child. There is also a higher incidence of still-births among women who smoke.

What lasting effects can maternal smoking cause an infant?

Once the infant is placed in a nonsmoking environment, the infant's health should improve. Initially, the infant may experience some nicotine withdrawal, characterized by irritability and fussiness. Unlike cocaine and alcohol, cigarette smoking does not cause mental retardation in infants.

Autism

Autism is a rare mental disorder. It can be present at birth or may become evident during the first thirty months of a child's life. Only about four children out of every ten thousand live births are autistic.

Autistic children appear physically well developed, yet show an inability to comprehend or to communicate verbally. Half of these children are either mute or unable to talk intelligibly. They tend to isolate themselves, and often act aloof and detached. They appear unaware of the people or world around them. Many of these children will have metabolic and neurologic defects.

So far, drug treatment for autism has not proven effective. Strict and purposeful behavior modification programs are currently reaping the most results. The children are taught subjects in small increments. A child giving an appropriate response receives an immediate reward.

Are many autistic children adopted?
No. Most autistic children are placed in institutions. Their behavioral difficulties as well as their inability to communicate with others makes caring for these children more of a challenge than many parents feel they are able to handle.

Cleft Lip and Cleft Palate

Cleft lip is a genetic birth defect occurring in one out of every one thousand live births. It is found more commonly in males. Cleft lip is a condition in which the upper lip does not close during fetal development. The gash or split can occur on one or both sides of the lip.

Cleft palate is the result of incomplete fusion of tissue or bone in the roof (palate) of the mouth. Like cleft lip, it can occur on one or both sides of the bony palate. Cleft palate occurs once in every 2,500 births and is more common in females. Surgical intervention to repair the lip and/or palate is necessary and may be started when the infant is one week old.

Infants with a cleft lip or palate typically experience some degree of feeding problems. They are often labeled "poor feeders" due to the difficulty they have in obtaining a good seal on the nipple of a bottle combined with an inadequate sucking reflex. Caregivers need to pay extra attention to ensure the infants receive enough nutrients.

Many infants experience difficulty breathing, which worsens when they try to eat. They tire quickly due to the extra energy they must expend to perform the simple tasks of eating and breathing.

Ear infections also are a common problem among children with cleft lips or palates. If these infections go untreated, the result can be permanent hearing loss.

Do all children with these conditions have speech problems?
No. A child with a cleft lip may or may not have any speech difficulties. However, speech problems always occur in children with cleft palates. A majority of these defects can be overcome with speech therapy.

What precautions should be taken when feeding one of these children?
The child should be cradled in an upright position in your arms. Special nipples have been designed to facilitate the infant's ability to eat, and to reduce the likelihood of choking. Allow the infant frequent rest periods during mealtime. If the infant is having trouble breathing, stop the feeding. Use a suction bulb to remove any formula in the mouth and

nose, and allow the infant to rest for about five minutes before continuing. Stop and burp the infant frequently during the feeding. This will remove excess air from the stomach and allow the infant to breathe easier. It is dangerous to feed *any* infant while he or she is lying flat. The danger of choking is even greater in an infant with a cleft lip or palate than a normal child.

My wife and I are considering adopting a five-year-old boy whose cleft lip has not been repaired. Is he too old to begin reconstructive surgery?
Although most children will begin to undergo the repair process shortly after birth and will continue the process into adolescence, reconstructive surgery can be started at virtually any age. Unrepaired cleft lips are more common in children adopted from foreign countries. Many countries cannot afford the cost of the repeated surgeries a child with a cleft lip or palate would require.

Are there any emotional difficulties associated with having a cleft lip or palate?
Emotional trauma is quite often the greatest problem a child with a cleft lip or palate will face. Other children can and will make fun of the child's facial appearance and speech difficulties. Helping your child to foster a positive self-image will allow him or her to cope with the remarks that others make. Some children benefit greatly from counsel, while others do fine without any outside intervention.

Are there any organizations that can give me further information about these conditions?
Yes. Call or write to the following:

The Cleft Palate Foundation
1218 Grandview Avenue
Pittsburgh, PA 15211
(412) 481-1376 or 1-800-24-CLEFT

Sickle-Cell Anemia

Sickle-cell anemia, or sickle-cell disease, is a genetic disease in which the oxygen-carrying red blood cells form an abnormal sickle shape. These cells block tiny blood vessels in the body, causing a condition known as sickle-cell crisis. Approximately sixty thousand African Americans suffer from sickle-cell anemia.

The symptoms of sickle-cell anemia include the following:

- Sores appear around the ankles or legs and do not heal as a result of poor circulation.
- Hand-foot syndrome is seen frequently in children with sickle-cell anemia. The small blood vessels become blocked, and the hands and feet begin to swell and become hot, red, and painful.
- Children with sickle-cell anemia are usually small in stature.
- People with this disease experience poor general health. They are prone to frequent colds and sore throats.
- Some people may have a yellowish tinge to the whites of their eyes. This indicates jaundice caused by the abnormal blood condition.
- Joint pain, especially in the shoulders and hips, is common.
- Sickle-cell crisis is the most common symptom of sickle-cell anemia.

Even though sickle cells are present at birth, the symptoms occur usually after six months of age.

Are these symptoms proof that a child has sickle-cell anemia?
No. Some of these symptoms can be caused by conditions other than sickle-cell anemia. Consult your physician for a diagnosis if you suspect that your child has sickle-cell anemia. The symptoms are not always apparent in people with a very mild form of the disease.

Does sickle-cell disease primarily affect African Americans?
In the U.S. today, sickle-cell anemia primarily affects African Americans. It can occur also in individuals who originate from the Caribbean, Latin America, Mediterranean or Middle Eastern areas, Southeast Asia, or India. Parents adopting children from any country in which sickle-cell anemia is commonly found should have their children tested.

What is a sickle-cell crisis?
Sickle-cell crisis occurs when large numbers of sickle cells stick together in the blood vessels, reducing the flow of oxygen in the body. It is characterized by severe pain in the chest, abdomen, arms, and legs. A sickle-cell crisis may last hours or weeks, and it can occur several times a year. Medical attention and intervention is usually required.

What is the treatment for sickle-cell anemia?
The treatment involves medications to relieve pain, antibiotics for the prevention of infection, increased fluid intake, and bed rest. Blood transfusions may be necessary.

What can we do to help our daughter cope with this illness?
All high risk children should be tested for the disease early.

This allows the physician to prescribe medications to minimize the threat of infections and relieve pain. Maintaining good general health with a proper diet, rest, and moderate exercise can help prevent sickle-cell crisis. Your daughter will tire easily. At times you may observe her pushing herself too hard, trying to keep up with the activities of other children. Plan rest periods to help her avoid fatigue. Bear in mind, however, that children with sickle-cell anemia are not invalids. Allow your daughter to participate in nonstrenuous activities. Try to help her avoid the stress of colds and upset stomachs. Also, pay special attention to the care of her skin. Help her to avoid infections from cuts and bruises by teaching her good personal hygiene.

Cystic Fibrosis

Cystic fibrosis is a genetic disease found most commonly in Caucasians. Children who have this disease produce large amounts of thick mucus in the respiratory tract, making breathing difficult and oxygen consumption compromised. As the disease progresses, these children develop barrel-shaped chests and clubbing of the fingers and toes. Often they will appear strikingly undernourished. In 80 percent of these children the pancreas is affected by the disease. Their abdomens may be distended, and they will have frequent and foul stools. Most children with cystic fibrosis are given oral vitamins to combat vitamin deficiencies, and daily physical therapy. Many children require oxygen therapy.

Is cystic fibrosis fatal?
Cystic fibrosis is a debilitating and fatal disease. Fifty percent of the children will live to be ten years old. Thirty percent

will reach the age of twenty, and twenty percent will live to be thirty years old.

Can cystic fibrosis be cured?
There is no cure at present. Treatment is directed toward the relief of symptoms.

Do children with cystic fibrosis require a special diet?
Yes. These children are placed on high-calorie, high-protein, moderate-fat diets. A double dose of vitamins is given daily, and pancreatic extract is given with each meal.

Our adopted son has cystic fibrosis. Should we limit his activities?
It is important for your son's well-being that you treat him as normal whenever possible. Allow him to exercise and play according to his individual tolerance. If your son is school age, he should attend regular classes as often as his physical health permits.

Muscular Dystrophy

Muscular dystrophy (MD) is a genetic disease affecting the skeletal muscle of the body. It usually begins in the preschool years, but it can begin in older children. A child with MD will appear physically normal until he or she begins to walk. Typical characteristics of the disease include flat feet, weakness in the legs, and an inability for the child to climb stairs or to walk without falling.

Children with MD will begin using a wheelchair sometime between the ages of seven and ten; most of these children must use a wheelchair by the time they are thirteen years old.

Is muscular dystrophy a fatal disease?

MD is a progressive disease. Few children live beyond twenty years of age. The most frequent causes of death can be attributed to respiratory infections (pneumonia) and heart-related complications.

How would we care for a child who has MD?

Your goal as a parent is to keep your child as independent and self-reliant as possible. Encourage your child to continue his or her normal activities. Your child can continue many daily activities independently with careful planning and modifications in clothing, feeding utensils, and equipment that he or she may require for bathing and for using the toilet. Light braces can be fitted for your child's legs to provide support to weakened muscles. Electric wheelchairs allow children with upper-extremity weakness to be independently mobile.

In managing your child's diet, it is important to prevent obesity, a frequent problem resulting from inactivity.

Diabetes

Diabetes mellitus is a genetically determined illness. It results in a lifetime of insufficient production of insulin, which leaves a person's body unable to utilize carbohydrates. Children with juvenile diabetes require daily injections of insulin to maintain normal bodily functions.

Symptoms which indicate a child may have some insulin deficiencies include increased appetite and calorie consumption with weight loss, excessive thirst, frequent urination, fatigue, nausea, vomiting, skin infections, blurred vision, and frequent bladder infections.

There is no known cure for diabetes at this time. The treatment for diabetes includes a life-style of care and management of the disease and its symptoms. Injections of insulin are given daily to control the blood glucose ("sugar") levels. A nutritious and carefully controlled diet plays a key role in diabetes management. A regular exercise program can improve the overall health of the diabetic. Many diabetic patients have experienced reductions in their daily insulin requirements after establishing an exercise program. *Note:* A good birthfamily history can alert adoptive parents to potential health risks of their adopted child.

Are diabetic children born with this disease?
Diabetes can occur at any time during childhood for children with a genetic predisposition to the illness. However, other poorly understood factors influence whether or not a person develops diabetes.

Do all children with diabetes require insulin injections?
The majority of children diagnosed with diabetes before they are nineteen years old require daily injections of insulin. They are called insulin-dependent diabetics.

How can I help my diabetic daughter to better manage this disease?
Encourage your daughter to express her feelings about her disease. If she can develop a realistic understanding of her disease, she will have fewer emotional adjustments.

  If your daughter is an older child, a nurse can teach her how to test her glucose levels and administer her own insulin injections. This will help her feel that she controls her disease instead of feeling like the disease controls her. Children frequently find themselves "caught in the moment" and may forget to take their medicine when it is needed. Therefore, be sure that your daughter wears a Medic-

Alert bracelet at all times. Teach your child to assume responsibility for the management of her illness.

Provide nutritious meals and snacks at regularly scheduled intervals, without extended periods of time between meals and snacks. Since infection increases the body's demand for insulin, avoid situations that are likely to increase your child's risk of infection. Teach your child how to maintain good skin care.

Cerebral Palsy

Cerebral palsy (CP) is any impairment of the brain affecting voluntary muscle movement (arms, legs, trunk, and eyes). The impairment is acquired before birth or during the early years of a child's development.

CP can be divided into four classifications:

- **Spastic:** The affected muscles are tense and subject to spasms
- **Athetoid:** There is uncontrollable muscle movement, including jerking and twitching
- **Ataxia:** The person experiences a loss of balance and an inability to control voluntary muscle movements
- **Tremor:** The affected limbs move in rhythmic and repetitive motions

Will a child with CP be mentally challenged?
CP affects muscle control; it does not affect a person's intelligence.

Is CP a progressive disease?
No. Cerebral palsy is not a condition that progressively worsens, and no additional brain damage occurs. The effects

of CP on a child's body will continue to change through the years. It is important that the child's need for physical therapy, orthopedic appliances, and speech and language therapy be evaluated and updated continually.

What additional problems might a child with CP have?

Most children with CP are quite healthy, and grow to lead happy, normal, productive lives. Half of the people who have CP may not speak or may have poor, ineffectual speech. Hearing difficulties can lead to a delay in the development of language skills in many of these children.

Some children with CP have a difficult time chewing and swallowing. These children need careful preparation of their food to help keep them from choking.

Visual disturbances requiring corrective intervention such as crossed eyes are common. Emotional as well as learning disabilities occur in a few children with CP. Some children will require drug therapy for seizures and tremors.

Orthopedic surgery is used to correct local physical defects. However, it is important to note that surgery will only improve limb function; it will not make the affected limbs normal.

Epilepsy

What is epilepsy?

Epilepsy is a general term used to describe recurring seizures or a loss or impairment of consciousness. Persons who have epilepsy can often control the severity and frequency of their seizures with medications.

Can epilepsy be cured?

No. Epilepsy is a lifelong illness with no known cure. There has been a great deal of success in controlling seizures with the use of certain medications. Many epileptic persons can maintain a normal life-style.

Is epilepsy contagious?
No. Epilepsy is not contagious. It is the result of a brain dysfunction that occurs either before birth or after a severe head injury. It cannot be transmitted to others.

Is epilepsy caused by insanity?
Throughout history people with epilepsy have been stigmatized and have often become outcasts of society. They have been branded as insane, stupid, mentally retarded, and possessed by evil spirits for many centuries, and even today some of these attitudes persist. There is no research to date indicating that those who are plagued with mental disorders are more likely to have epileptic seizures. Similarly, there is no evidence suggesting a higher incidence of mental disorders in people with epilepsy than in the community at large.

Are children with epilepsy mentally retarded?
Mental retardation is not found with this disease. However, if a child has a life-threatening seizure which continues for several minutes leaving the child unable to breathe, the resulting lack of oxygen to the brain may cause some permanent brain damage.

I have heard that various types of seizures are associated with epilepsy. What are they?
There are four basic epileptic seizure classifications. We will address the two most common:

- **Grand mal seizures** are abrupt, generalized seizures. People who have this type of seizure describe a peculiar feeling, sight, sound, smell, taste, or twitching immediately preceding the onset of a seizure. This sensation is called an aura. The person falls to the ground, loses consciousness, and becomes pale. The eyes roll upward, and the head is thrown backward or to the side. The person may bite his or her tongue during a seizure and may urinate or defecate uncontrollably. When the seizure has ended, the person sleeps.

- **Petit mal seizures**, sometimes called absence spells, develop after a child is three years of age, and frequently disappear once a child reaches adolescence. During this type of seizure the child may appear to be staring or daydreaming. There is no noticeable movement in some children; others have a slight fluttering of the eyelids or a faint twitching of the hand. The child stops what he or she is doing at the beginning of a seizure and then automatically resumes the task immediately following the seizure, with no recollection of the episode.

What is the medical treatment for epilepsy?

Antiseizure medications are used to control or reduce seizure activity in 75 percent of the people diagnosed with grand mal seizures. Ninety percent of the children with petit mal seizures have no seizures or have greatly reduced seizure activity when they take antiseizure medications.

What are the side effects of antiseizure medications?

Your child may experience drowsiness, restlessness, rash, up-set stomach, fatigue, or dizziness as a result of the medications. Never discontinue a medication without first consulting your physician.

Will a child with epilepsy take medication his or her entire life?

If the child goes one year without any seizure activity, the epilepsy is considered controlled. At that time your physician may begin weaning your child from the medication. If the seizures return, your child will require additional medication treatment.

What can we do to decrease the number of seizures our child has?

Maintaining your child on a routine medication schedule is of the utmost importance. Other measures include reducing stress, avoiding loud noises or blinking lights, and developing a solid, supportive family unit.

Chapter 9

INTERNATIONAL MEDICAL CONSIDERATIONS

Many children in foreign countries are housed in orphanages, refugee camps, and government institutions—some even live on the streets. There are certain health issues a prospective adoptive parent of a foreign child should consider. A great many of the illnesses are correctable with the proper medical intervention of a knowledgeable pediatrician.

We need to find a pediatrician for the child we are planning to adopt from Korea. Should we choose a doctor now, or wait until we have returned with our child?
There can be unforeseen difficulties involved in an international adoption. Typically, the first weeks following your return home are hectic and unsettled. You do not want to face a situation in which your child becomes ill and you must frantically scramble to find a pediatrician. Plan ahead. Talk

with other parents, interview several physicians, and pick the one who will best serve your needs. Some physicians require advance notice before they will take new patients. Check with your physician to see if he or she is taking new patients. Make an appointment for a medical exam for your child shortly after his or her arrival in the U.S.

What qualities should we look for when choosing a pediatrician?

Interviewing a physician—which you can do by phone—is an important first step to help you in your search. During your interview determine the physician's views on adoption. Choose a physician who believes adoption is a positive way to build a family. Ask about his or her experiences in the recognition and treatment of commonly found illnesses in foreign-born children (malnutrition, TB, hepatitis).

What health problems might we expect to see in foreign-born children?

Non-life-threatening health problems your child may have can include any of the following:

- Intestinal parasites
- Lice
- Skin rashes or scars
- Scabies
- Food intolerance or food allergies
- Lactose (milk) intolerance
- Overeating or poor appetite
- Poor muscle tone
- Sleep disturbances
- Ear infections
- Urinary tract infections

Warning: Do not give your child any medication until you have consulted your child's pediatrician.

What health regulations does U.S. Immigrations place on orphans entering the U.S. through adoption?

The U.S. Immigration and Naturalization Service requires all immigrants, including orphans, entering the U.S. to undergo a complete health examination:

- All immigrants regardless of age must have a general physical exam. This exam must be completed before a visa is issued. Prospective parents are urged to get psychological as well as medical evaluations for their adopted child. The exams should be performed by professionals who are recommended by the U.S Embassy or Consulate.
- A specific exam for the signs and symptoms of AIDS as well as a blood test for HIV is required. Any exam or test the physician believes is necessary to rule out any dangerous infections will be required.
- In addition to the other required exams, immigrants fifteen years old and older must have a chest X-ray and a blood test for sexually transmitted diseases.

Where will the test for AIDS be performed? Should we be concerned about the accuracy of these tests in foreign countries?

No. The U.S. Embassy or Consulate decides which AIDS testing facility they will work with in each foreign country. The facilities as well as personnel working in them have been approved by U.S.-trained physicians on U.S. Embassy staffs to ensure accurate test results. In countries without testing facilities, regional testing centers have been established by the U.S. Testing Center for Asia.

What is the minimal medical information that I will need in order to adopt a foreign child?

- Every child must have a physical examination. Request a written explanation of any abnormalities, and the recommended treatments. If the child is less than one year old, the physical exam must be given within the one or two months before the adoption. If the child is one to five years of age, the exam must be given within the six months prior to the adoption. A child who is five years of age or older must have a physical exam within the year prior to the adoption. *Note:* Any child with a change in medical status should have an examination within two months of the adoption. After two months it may be difficult or even impossible to acquire the medical information you need.
- You must have evidence of the child's birth date or estimated birth date. A copy of the original birth certificate is best. If that cannot be obtained, ask how the child's age or date of birth was determined.
- Request the child's current height and weight. Ask whether pounds and inches were used, or kilograms and centimeters.
- Ask the physician, adoption agency, or orphanage director for a growth and development assessment. Ask how your child compares to the other children of his or her age in the same environment, whether it is an orphanage, a government institution, or a foster home. This will give you a more accurate and realistic idea of your child's development.
- All children under two years old must be measured for head circumference. This alerts your physician in the U.S. to any possibility of hydrocephalus (an enlargement of the head) or microcephaly (abnormal smallness of the

head). Either condition may indicate a certain degree of mental retardation in a child.

- Ask for documentation of any immunizations your adopted child has received. Many foreign-born children have never received any of the childhood vaccinations Americans often take for granted.
- Ask your in-country contact or agency for all available information concerning the birthmother's pregnancy and delivery. Request that any known information pertaining to the birthfamily be included in the report.
- A list of all illnesses, hospitalizations, injuries, and medical treatments, as well as current medicines and medication allergies, can prove invaluable when you are trying to piece together a viable and accurate medical history.
- Your physician in the U.S. will need an in-depth description of any medical treatments your child is currently undergoing. This information will allow your physician to determine the best plan of care for your child, and will indicate which medical treatments, if any, have proved unsuccessful.
- *Special note:* Unfortunately much of the medical information you receive may be inaccurate if it is available at all. Take your child to a pediatrician within a week of his or her arrival to the U.S. for a more accurate diagnosis of the child's existing medical condition.

What medical tests are recommended for our Vietnamese daughter once she enters the U.S.?
According to the International Adoption Clinic at the University of Minnesota in Minneapolis, there are at least seven screening tests any foreign-born child should receive from his or her pediatrician during the first two weeks following your child's arrival in the U.S.:

1. A hepatitis B profile, which includes testing for hepatitis B surface antigens, and antibodies to hepatitis B, as well as core antigens.
2. A Mantoux test (an intradermal skin test) with Candida control, to determine tuberculosis. If the child received the BCG vaccine, a chest X-ray may be necessary to diagnose TB.
3. A fecal examination for intestinal ova and parasites. This should be done once a month for six months. Some parasites take as long as six months to show up.
4. A urinalysis for any urinary tract infection, and a urine culture for the presence of cytomegalovirus.
5. Complete and thorough vision and hearing tests. The vision test should include a slitlamp and funduscopic examination by an ophthalmologist.
6. A complete blood cell count with erythrocyte indexes.
7. A Venereal Disease Research Laboratories (VDRL) series for any sexually transmitted diseases, in the event that your child, especially an older child, has suffered some form of sexual abuse.

Note: The diseases your child may have been exposed to are an expression of the environment that the child has been raised in and not an indicator of his or her morality.

Nutritional Deficiency Diseases

Children need nourishing diets for proper growth and development. In developing countries, nutritional deficiencies account for a great many of the health problems seen in children today. Diets in developing countries are often low in protein. The majority of calories are obtained from irregular meals, which usually have low vitamin and high starch content. Malnutrition can be a common problem in foreign-born children.

What are the symptoms of malnutrition?

Malnourished children are likely to display the following symptoms:

1. Malnourished children usually grow at a slower rate than children receiving healthy, well-balanced diets. These children may experience developmental delays resulting in physical and mental stunting.
2. They are severely underweight for their age and size.
3. Their skin is dry and sometimes flaky, and the skin color may be pale or ashy.
4. They will have dry, brittle, lackluster hair which may be sparse and falling out.
5. Because their immune systems are affected, they are susceptible to infection.
6. They may have diarrhea. Remember diarrhea left untreated in infants and toddlers can lead to death by dehydration.

What can we do for our adopted child who appears malnourished?

A pediatrician should evaluate your child, then a diet can be tailored for the child's specific nutritional needs. Most children will need to start with a diet low in seasonings and spices. A multivitamin will begin to replenish the necessary minerals and vitamins in the child's body. Offer frequent small servings of meals and snacks.

Your child's health and well-being depend on his or her nutritional status. Do not treat malnutrition without consulting your pediatrician. Severe malnutrition may require the child to be hospitalized. Intravenous (through the vein) feedings, antibiotics for any infection, or medicine to control diarrhea may be necessary. **Warning:** Do not give your child any medication until you have consulted your child's pediatrician.

What are some specific vitamin deficiencies I might expect to see in my foreign-born daughter?

If your daughter is from Asia or a country in which the typical diet consists mainly of rice, she may have a vitamin B_1 or thiamine deficiency. If her diet consisted mainly of corn or maize, she may have a niacin deficiency. She may also be anemic; iron deficiency is common in countries where the typical diet is low in protein or is virtually protein free.

A vitamin A deficiency can lead to ulceration of the cornea. If left untreated, it will eventually cause blindness. Rickets, a childhood disease caused by a vitamin D deficiency, results in the softening of bones. Deformities often result in the weight-bearing bones. A bowing of the legs is common in those who are severely affected.

Scurvy is a disease caused by a vitamin C deficiency. The symptoms include loosening of teeth, joint and bone pain, and bleeding of the tiny blood vessels beneath the surface of the skin. Vitamin C is a water-soluble vitamin that cannot be stored in the human body; therefore, vitamin C should be consumed daily. Excess amounts of the vitamin are excreted through the kidneys. Sources of vitamin C include citrus fruit, tomatoes, cabbage, potatoes, strawberries, and melons.

Children in countries with nonfluoridated water will experience varying degrees of tooth decay.

Intestinal Parasites

Intestinal parasites refer to the infestation of round-worms, ringworms, pinworms, and/or tapeworms. Infestation begins with fecal-contaminated soil, water, or food.

The symptoms of intestinal parasites include chronic

diarrhea, blood-streaked stools, colicky pain, weight loss, and/or bloating.

If you have recently adopted a child who may have one of these parasites, the nutritional well-being of your child depends on the correct diagnosis of the type of worm your child carries. A microscopic examination of stool specimens will allow your physician to determine the specific medications necessary for treatment. **Warning:** Do not give your child any medication until you have consulted your child's pediatrician.

Which children need to be screened for intestinal parasites?
We recommend that all children from countries outside the U.S. receive screening for parasites, especially those who have been abandoned prior to placement in a hospital or orphanage. Others who need to be screened are children with symptoms of chronic diarrhea, unexplained weight loss, or bloating. Any child who has been treated for intestinal parasites needs a repeat stool examination. Stool specimens should be checked once a month for six months upon your return to the U.S. This ensures your child is not harboring long-incubating parasites.

Enteritis

Enteritis is an inflammation of the intestines. It is caused by viral or bacterial infections, food allergies, or toxins. The symptoms of enteritis include abdominal pain, nausea, vomiting, and diarrhea.

Infants and toddlers who have enteritis are treated with a diet of clear liquids or diluted formula. Older children are treated with a liquid or bland diet. All infected children must avoid any foods causing allergic reactions which trigger diarrhea or vomiting. Antibiotics, antidiarrheal, or antiemetic (arresting vomiting) medications, as well as pain medicine, may be prescribed.

Cases of severe diarrhea and vomiting may require the elimination of all food and liquids given by mouth, and replacement with intravenous (through the vein) feedings. Hospitalization is necessary for this treatment. Dehydration in children caused by vomiting and diarrhea can be life-threatening. Please contact your physician immediately.

Lactose Intolerance

Lactose intolerance occurs in infants and children unable to tolerate cow's milk or milk products. Children who suffer from lactose intolerance may experience diarrhea, vomiting, or excessive and uncomfortable gas production in the intestines.

As a parent, you can choose to completely eliminate all milk and milk products from your child's diet. You must discuss with your pediatrician the best way to supplement your child's diet thus ensuring he or she receives the essential nutrients—calcium, phosphorus, and vitamin D—found in milk and other dairy products.

Is there anything we can do other than completely eliminate milk and milk products from the diet of a child who is lactose intolerant?
Yes. There are a few commercial products on the market today that ease the uncomfortable side effects of lactose intolerance. These products are trademarked as Lactaid and Dairy Ease. They can be bought over the counter in tablet or liquid form. Many milk companies offer milk to which the enzyme acidophilus has been added. This enzyme breaks down lactose, making the milk easier to digest.

Which children are most likely to show signs of lactose intolerance?

Children of Asian heritage are frequently lactose intolerant. Infants raised on vegetable-based formulas as well as on other milk such as goat's milk, may also exhibit signs of intolerance to milk-based formulas.

What is the best way to manage the feedings of a milk-intolerant infant?

Lactose-intolerant infants will require a soybean-based formula. Two such formulas are listed under the trademark Isomil and ProSobee. Ask your pediatrician to recommend an infant formula to fit your baby's needs.

We have heard of infants who experience difficulty in adjusting to American baby formulas. What can we do to help our child adjust?

Most foreign infant formulas are vegetable-based formulas that contain large amounts of sugar to improve the taste and to provide additional calories. American formulas do not use sugar to add calories. If your infant does not like the taste of American formulas, there may be a simple solution. If your infant does not have diarrhea or an intestinal illness, you can add up to a tablespoon of light corn syrup to an eight-ounce bottle of formula. This will increase the sweetness, and it is easily digestible. *Note:* Corn syrup may cause your infant to have loose stools, which means it can remedy constipation. **Do not use table sugar or honey;** both of these can harm your infant.

What products contain lactose?

Lactose is a milk sugar; therefore, it is found in all milk and milk products, such as yogurt, ice cream, sour cream, all cheeses, and whipped cream.

INTERNATIONAL MEDICAL CONSIDERATIONS

Food Intolerance

Food intolerance is an inability to tolerate particular foods. Children raised in foreign orphanages and institutions are fed bland diets. Your child's digestive system may be unprepared for the rich or spicy foods that we Americans consume daily. A child may experience vomiting, diarrhea, or constipation if these foods are introduced too quickly or in large amounts.

The treatment for food intolerance is simple. Provide your child with a nutritious but bland diet. If the child does not have food allergies, iron- and vitamin-fortified hot cereals made of creamed rice, creamed wheat, malt, or oats are excellent sources of nutrition. They also provide tastes and textures that your child may find familiar. Gradually introduce one new food at a time into the child's diet. This will give you the opportunity to identify any food allergies.

Food Allergy

Food allergy refers to an allergic reaction that can be attributed to a specific food. The child who has a food allergy may break out in a fine red rash or welts. Other symptoms include itching, red or watering eyes, and draining or congested sinuses. Life-threatening reactions include swelling of the lips and throat, which restricts the ability to breathe.

To treat food allergies, completely eliminate all foods to which your child shows any sensitivity. Ask your pediatrician to recommend any vitamin, mineral, or protein supplements your child will need. Reintroduce foods slowly.

We have noticed our six-year-old son from Honduras is hiding food around the house. We seem unable to stop this habit. What can we do?

Your son probably comes from an environment in which food was scarce and meals were small. His habit of hoarding and hiding food is a self-protective means against starvation. After years of deprivation, he cannot comprehend the concept of always having enough to eat.

You can try explaining to your son that he will always have food, but don't expect his behavior to change drastically. You may want to leave a few fruits and healthy snacks within easy reach. Allow him to pick the foods he likes as frequently as possible, and begin teaching him to distinguish whether or not he is actually hungry. Note, however, that some parents report that their children continue to hoard food no matter what they do.

Our daughter, whom we adopted from a Korean orphanage, refuses to eat anything except cream of rice or boiled rice. How can we encourage her to try other foods?

Begin helping your daughter adjust to new and different foods by slowly introducing them into her diet. If she is an older child and resistant to trying new foods, you may have to tell her that she must at least taste one bite of any new food. To encourage fruits, start adding jellies, jams, or preserves to her rice cereal. If you have older children in the family, call your daughter's attention to any positive eating habits they have.

We have adopted a baby boy from Colombia. His arrival has been delayed due to a viral infection that is causing diarrhea. Should we be alarmed? And will he need additional medical intervention once he arrives?

Diarrhea in children can be serious if it is left untreated. Diarrhea is not a disease; it can be caused by a reaction to certain foods, infections, or illnesses.

The severity of the diarrhea determines the course of treatment. Diarrhea in infants is dangerous because it can rapidly lead to dehydration. Infants who have diarrhea may need hospitalization for treatment with intravenous fluids or antibiotics. Your son should be seen by his pediatrician within twenty-four hours of arrival in the U.S. The pediatrician will determine the treatment your son needs. **Warning:** Do not give your child any medication until you have consulted your child's pediatrician.

Salmonella

Salmonella is a bacterial infection affecting the stomach and intestines. It is a mild disease to which young children under the age of five are vulnerable. It is easily transmissible to others. The symptoms of salmonellosis include nausea, vomiting, diarrhea, fever, and severe abdominal pain that will last several days. A child can continue to excrete the bacteria causing salmonella for up to two months after the initial infection. Salmonella is frequently excreted in the stools of children raised in unsanitary conditions.

Salmonella is transmitted most commonly through contaminated food—eggs, meat, shellfish, or milk. Direct transmission can occur also from household pets such as dogs, cats, parakeets, and turtles.

How can we determine the presence of salmonella in our child if there are no symptoms?
A stool culture can easily detect the presence of salmonella and can be done at your pediatrician's office.

If our child has salmonella, what precautions are necessary?
Properly dispose of stools and diapers, and wash your hands thoroughly—preferably with an antibacterial soap—before handling or preparing any food.

Diseases of the Skin

Lice

Lice are external parasites that live on the body, hair, and clothing of the infected person. Lice are tiny, gray bugs that hop and lay egg cases, called nits, in body hair. The egg cases look like dandruff and are stuck to the hair shaft. A person may become infested with lice through direct contact with others who have them or through contact with infested towels, clothing, linens, or hair. Pubic lice can be acquired by these same methods but may be transmitted by toilet seats.

Lice treatments can be bought over the counter without a prescription. We recommend Nix (permethrin) shampoo because it is safe to use on children of all ages. However, the combs found in lice kits are ineffective for the removal of nits. They must be pulled off one at a time.

How many children from orphanages have lice?
Lice infestations are found in the majority of children living in foreign orphanages and institutions. The overcrowded and unsanitary conditions provide a breeding ground for all skin parasites.

How can we determine if our child has lice, and how do we treat our child for lice if we find some?
Look for the dandruff-size nits on the scalp behind the ears and around the nape of the neck. If you see the tiny, gray,

bugs or any egg cases, wash your child's hair thoroughly. Next, add the Nix the same way you would add a cream rinse. Wait ten to fifteen minutes, and then rinse. Although this treatment is about 99 percent effective, we recommend that you give your child a second treatment ten days later. Wash all bedding and clothing, and run it through a hot dryer; the heat kills the eggs, thus preventing reinfestation. Gather all the stuffed animals in your house together, and seal them in a large plastic garbage bag for at least one week. It is not necessary to treat rugs, carpets, or furniture.

Should our future adopted son be treated for lice routinely?
It takes two weeks after initial infestation for lice to hatch from eggs. When you bring your son home, we recommend that you treat him with Nix as a precautionary measure. You do not need to continue the treatment once it has been determined he is not infested.

If we cannot find the product Nix, how can we treat our child for lice?
There are many good lice treatment products available without a prescription at most drugstores. Your pharmacist can recommend the products safe for your child's use. The use of a product depends on the age of your child.

Scabies
Scabies is a skin infestation of mites, characterized by red, itchy lesions (sores) and intense itching at night. Scabies is commonly found on children living in the unsanitary and overcrowded conditions associated with foreign orphanages or refugee camps.

There is a new and safe drug on the market called Elimite (permethrin 5 percent cream). It can be obtained only with a prescription. If your child has scabies, apply Elimite to your child from head to toe at bedtime. Do not wash it off until the following morning. You can repeat the application in ten to fourteen days, but it can be repeated only once.

All bedding and clothing should be washed the same day you wash the Elimite off your child. Heat will kill the mites on personal items. Gather all stuffed toys, coats, linens, and pillows, and run them through a hot dryer. If some of these items cannot be put into a dryer, place them in a tightly sealed plastic bag and leave for two weeks. Vacuuming rugs and furniture will sufficiently eliminate any stray mites.

How can we determine whether or not our daughter has scabies?
If your daughter has red, itchy lesions or sores and you are unsure of the cause, take her to a dermatologist. The dermatologist can scrape a lesion and view it under a microscope to determine whether mites are present.

Our son, whom we adopted from Romania, has been treated for scabies, but the sores will not go away. Is there something else we can try?
The lesions or sores may remain long after the mites are dead. The sores are an allergic reaction to the waste products deposited by the scabies. You can apply a hydrocortisone cream to the sores. If your son does not receive much relief, ask his physician to recommend an antihistamine that you can give your son by mouth.

Impetigo
Impetigo is a skin infection caused by bacteria and characterized by crusty scab-like lesions on the face, scalp, arms, and legs. Impetigo is contagious, and spreads rapidly

by direct contact with infected persons. It is commonly found in countries with warm, humid climates, and in southern U.S. states during the summer. It can be readily seen in children suffering from malnutrition or poor hygiene, or living in overcrowded conditions.

Oral antibiotics given three to four times a day for a full seven to ten days are very effective for treating impetigo. A single shot of penicillin is equally effective. Scratching the lesions caused by the disease delays healing. If your child has impetigo, clip the child's fingernails short to discourage him or her from picking at and removing scabs. A calamine-based lotion will relieve the itching. Personal items such as towels, washcloths, and clothes should not be shared among family members. Impetigo is highly contagious.

Diseases of the Ear

Hearing defects are seen frequently in children from foreign countries. Chronic draining of the ears, untreated perforations in the eardrum, and auditory sequelae are the most common defects of the ears found in the children of most Third World countries.

Medical treatment in foreign orphanages is often nonexistent. Children with simple ear infections may go without treatment for years. The infections become chronic. As a result, permanent hearing loss can occur. There have been couples who have adopted a child they believed to be deaf. However, once the child received proper medical treatment in the U.S., much of the hearing loss was reversed. Usually the damage to the ears is extensive and deafness is permanent, especially in older children.

Middle-ear infections (otitis media) are quite common in infants and young children. They occur when fluid becomes trapped and collects behind the eardrum. Bacteria enter the ear through the throat or through a perforation in the eardrum, and pus forms. Left untreated, the eardrum may rupture as a result of the inflammation and pressure caused by the infection.

The symptoms of middle-ear infection can include irritability, a tendency to tug or rub the ears, high fever, runny nose and a cough, hearing loss, and sleep difficulties.

Middle-ear infections are treated with antibiotics that the child takes by mouth. A nonaspirin pain reliever such as Children's Tylenol may be given for the fever and discomfort associated with the infection. Some doctors recommend using nasal decongestants formulated especially for children. These decongestants will unblock the child's nasal passages and prevent the further build-up of fluid. **Warning:** Do not give your child any medication until you have consulted your child's pediatrician.

An agency from Mexico has contacted us about a two-year-old boy who is partially deaf. A preliminary medical report mentions "running ears." Is this a permanent condition?
No. Running or drainage from the ears indicates a perforation of the eardrums, which allows any fluid collecting in the middle ear to drain. The eardrum may be perforated as a result of infection, a sharp object introduced into the ear canal, or a loud blast of sound. Antibiotics are used to treat any infection in the ear. Severely damaged eardrums may require surgical intervention to remove scar tissue or to repair perforations.

Is the hearing loss associated with ear infections permanent?
Any child with a middle-ear infection will experience some degree of hearing loss, but it is usually temporary. The

ineffectual or nonexistent treatment of chronic ear infections can lead to varying degrees of deafness. A simple examination of the ear by your physician, along with a detailed hearing screening, can help determine the degree of deafness and the course of treatment your child needs.

Are deaf children mentally retarded?
Deafness is not an indication of a child's mental capabilities. Compromised hearing during the critical periods of language development, even for short periods of time, can affect a child's ability to communicate and to develop language skills. This may lead to the incorrect assumption that the child is mentally challenged.

Which children need hearing tests?
It is recommended that every child receive a hearing test. Early detection and treatment will prevent prolonged delays in language development and socialization skills.

How old must a child be in order to receive a hearing test?
Hearing tests are administered often in the newborn nurseries throughout the U.S. Age is a factor only when the physician must determine which type of hearing test to perform.

Age versus Size Discrepancies

People considering adoption usually have an idea about the age of the child they hope to begin parenting. Those adopting a foreign child must realize that malnutrition as well as a lack of stimulation can make a child smaller and developmentally slower than an American child of the same age.

A six-year-old child raised in an orphanage in South

America cannot be expected to be as developmentally advanced as a six-year-old American child. Rather than placing this child in the first grade, a year of nursery school followed by kindergarten will allow the child enough time to adjust to his or her new life-style and to develop language and socialization skills with children of similar size.

We are placing our five-year-old daughter in a nursery school this fall. She was adopted from an orphanage in India. We are concerned that the stigma of being "held back" will be a problem for her in the later grades. What can we do?

Your concern is understandable. You are trying to provide an environment in which your daughter can socialize while developing her language skills. Your concern lies in the fact that she will be older than the other children in her grade and that she may later be tagged as a learning-disabled student.

There is a simple solution. You can have your child's age legally changed on her birth certificate.

Note: Be careful when having your daughter's age legally changed. Poor records may have made her actual age uncertain. Some abandoned children in foreign countries do not have a record of birth. They are given an estimated birth date by the physicians or directors of their orphanages. It is common for these children, who have been raised in extreme poverty, to be smaller than average size. The sudden onset of puberty in a child whose age was estimated to be five or six years old can be a tremendous shock to adoptive parents. In situations like this, the child's age was grossly underestimated.

Visual Disturbances

Visual disturbances and blindness occur as a result of bacterial infections, nutritional diseases, transmission of diseases to an infant through the birth canal, or the oxygen therapy that premature infants receive.

Retinopathy of prematurity, or retrolental fibroplasia, occurs when premature infants are given high concentrations of oxygen for prolonged periods. To identify this condition, an ophthalmologist can perform a slitlamp funduscopic examination. Surgical intervention is quite effective in correcting visual problems caused by retrolental fibroplasia.

A regimen of oral antibiotics and antibiotic drops is used to treat infections of the eyes (conjunctivitis).

Dental Health

Dental health is frequently overlooked in children living in foreign orphanages. Many children have never brushed their teeth and as a result suffer from poor oral health. Extensive restorative work may be required to save a child's permanent teeth. Begin teaching your child dental hygiene immediately. It is recommended that your child see a dentist within the first month of arrival.

Chapter 10

ADOPTION RESOURCES

*R*esources are invaluable to the person or family who is interested in adopting a child. They can also be very difficult to locate for someone new to the world of adoption. If you have already searched, you have undoubtedly found that local bookstores and libraries are limited in their selections. Many resources are overwhelming and hard to get through. Others are hard to find. We have tried to take the frustration out of the resource search by providing you with some of the best adoption resources available today. Each listed resource will in turn guide you to other excellent resources. Use this chapter as a guide to map your way through the maze called adoption.

Adoption Resource Guides

National Adoption Directory, Washington, D.C., National Adoption Information Clearinghouse, 1992. Contains listings of adoption agencies, parent support groups, I.N.S. offices, and other adoption resources, as well as information on international adoption. The cost is twenty dollars, including postage. Order from National Adoption Information Clearinghouse, 1400 Eye Street, NW, Suite 600, Washington, DC 20005.

Posner, Julia. *The Adoption Resource Guide: A National Directory of Licensed Agencies*, Washington, D.C., Child Welfare League of America, 1990. Revised and expanded. This excellent book contains state listings of agencies, private-agency summary tables, out-of-state agencies, national agencies, national and regional adoption exchanges, additional licensed agencies, and information, referral, and support services. If it is not available at your local bookstore, write to Child Welfare League of America, 440 First Street, NW, Suite 310, Washington, DC 20001-2085.

National and Support Organizations

Aask America
Aid to Adoption to Special Kids
450 Sansome Street, Suite 210
San Francisco, CA 94111
(415) 434-2775 or (414) 781-4112

Aask America provides specialized services for special-needs children. They do the following:

- Place special-needs children in adoptive homes without fees to the adopting family
- Assist and encourage other licensed adoption agencies to place special-needs children

- Enable traditional and nontraditional families to successfully adopt special-needs children
- Provide national leadership to the field of adoption

Adoptive Families of America (AFA)
3307 Highway 100 North
Minneapolis, MN 55422
(612) 535-4829 (24-hour hotline)

AFA is a private, nonprofit membership organization of families and individuals that provides problem-solving assistance and information about the challenges of adoption to members of adoptive and prospective adoptive families. The organization creates opportunities for successful adoptive placement and promotes the health and welfare of children without permanent families. AFA publishes *Ours* magazine, which is a "must" for anyone interested in adoption. The AFA hotline can give you information about an emotional or medical problem, your child's behavior, the adoption of an older child, bonding adjustments, adoption disruptions, and how to find a good counselor, and it can provide answers to any general adoption questions.

American Adoption Congress (AAC)
Cherokee Station
P.O. Box 20137
New York, NY 10028-0051
(212) 988-0110
AAC Search Hotline: (505) 296-2198

AAC is a nonprofit, international educational network dedicated to promoting openness and honesty in adoption. They provide conferences, a national forum for search and support groups, a newsletter that provides an overview of current trends in the adoption movement, a bibliography of all adoption-related topics, and other services.

Child Welfare League of America (CWLA)
440 First Street, NW, Suite 310
Washington, DC 20001-2085
(202) 638-2952

CWLA is the largest privately supported, nonprofit organization in North America that devotes its efforts to helping deprived, neglected, and abused children and their families. They are also concerned with adoption, day care, adolescent pregnancy, and similar matters. They are strong advocates in Congress on the behalf of children. CWLA's library contains the most complete collection of materials related to child welfare in North America. You can request information and assistance from them on adoption.

Committee for Single Adoptive Parents, Inc.
P.O. Box 15084
Chevy Chase, MD 20815
(Mail inquiries only)

The Committee provides information and referral services to both prospective and actual single adoptive parents. They publish *The Handbook for Single Adoptive Parents*, by Hope Marindin (see the Bibliography).

International Concerns Committee for Children (ICCC)
911 Cyprus Drive
Boulder, CO 80303
(303) 494-8333

ICCC is a nonprofit, charitable and educational organization that provides nationwide services on information, advocacy, and referral to anyone interested in adoption and adoption agencies. They publish the annual *Report on Foreign Adoption* with monthly updates. For an annual twenty-five dollar donation you can receive a photo list of waiting children who live overseas as well as foreign-born children who have continued living in the U.S. after experiencing an adoption disruption.

Joint Council on International Children's Services
c/o Bruce M. Baehr
Americans for International Aid and Adoption
P.O. Box 290
Plainsville, NY 13137-0290
(315) 638-9449

      The Joint Council is an umbrella organization that unites parent groups, agencies, and individuals working in the field of international adoption. They promote ethical international adoption practices and advocacy for the rights of children. The Joint Council monitors legislation relating to international services; conducts an annual conference; publishes a quarterly journal, *The Bulletin*, updating the current issues and practices of international adoption; and provides public education on adoption issues.

National Adoption Information Clearinghouse (NAIC)
1400 Eye Street, NW, Suite 600
Washington, DC 20005
(301) 231-6512

      NAIC's purpose is to provide the public with easily accessible information on all aspects of infant and international adoption and the adoption of children with special needs. They publish a range of adoption materials including adoption directories, adoption resources, referrals to adoption experts, films and videotapes on adoption, and fact sheets on every aspect of adoption. There is no charge for the first copy of a resource you order and a minimal charge for additional copies of the same fact sheet. There is also a book on state adoption laws available from the NAIC for ten dollars. We highly recommend that you write or call for their catalog.

National Committee for Adoption
1930 Seventeenth Street NW
Washington, DC 20009-6207
(202) 328-1200
National Adoption Hotline: (202) 328-8072
    The National Committee for Adoption is a non-profit organization founded to strengthen adoption and related services. Their primary goal is to promote adoption as a positive option for young, single, or troubled parents. They publish the *Adoption Factbook* and some newsletters, provide a bookstore, provide coordination between national organizations and local service providers, and offer other important services. Their hotline can give you information and referral on maternity services, adoption resources, and infertility support groups in your area.

Free Adoption Information

    To receive either of the following free items, send your name and complete address to Adoptive Families of America, 3333 Highway 100 North, Minneapolis, MN 55422, (612) 535-4829.

Adoption Resources and Information. This free forty-eight-page booklet contains the following:

- In-depth information about 242 adoption agencies
- Resources for parents and children
- Information on independent, special-needs, and international adoption
- Tips on choosing an agency or an attorney
- A listing of 350 adoptive parent support groups

Free Subsidy Information. This is a free information packet explaining subsidies to families who are adopting children who were born in the U.S.

Parent Support Groups

National Resources for Locating Parent Support Groups

Adoptive Families of America
3333 Highway 110 North
Minneapolis, MN 55422
(612) 535-4829

Families Adopting Children Everywhere
P.O. Box 28058
Northwood Station
Baltimore, MD 21239
(301) 488-2656

Families for Private Adoption
P.O. Box 6375
Washington, DC 20015-0375
(202) 722-0338

Latin American Parents' Association
P.O. Box 72
Seaford, NY 11783

Committee for Single Adoptive Parents
P.O. Box 15084
Chevy Chase, MD 21239

The National Adoption Center
(For special-needs children)
1218 Chestnut Street
Philadelphia, PA 19107
(215) 925-0200

National Adoption Clearinghouse
Suite 410
11426 Rockville Pike
Rockville, MD 20852
(202) 842-1919

North American Council on Adoptable Children
1821 University Avenue, Suite N-498
St. Paul, MN 55104
(612) 644-3036

Adoptive Families of America Parent Support Groups

The following list includes some of the adoptive parent support groups that are group members of Adoptive Families of America (AFA). These support groups are listed by state to provide prospective and currently adoptive parents support in their area. All of these groups are helpful in sharing information with anyone who needs it, regardless of the person's state of residence. (For example, Kentucky does not have a support group for parents with Romanian children, so these parents may want to contact a support group in another state.) For a complete list of support groups, contact AFA at 3333 Highway 100 North, Minneapolis, MN 55422, (612) 535-4829.

Alaska
Anchorage Adoptive Parents' Association
Fred Getty
550 W. 7th, Suite 1780
Anchorage, AK 99502
(907) 248-4506

Alabama
Adoption Connection
Nann Worel
2620 Charlotte Oaks Drive
Mobile, AL 36695
(205) 661-4682

Alabama Friends of Adoption
Patrice Murphy
Box 131267
Birmingham, AL 35213
(205) 969-3510

Arkansas
Miracles
Connie Foster
1008 Barbara
Jacksonville, AR 35213
(501) 982-7134

River Valley Adoption Support Group
Elizabeth and Steve Franks
1005 W. 18th Terrace
Russellville, AR 72801
(501) 967-1641

California

ACCEPT (singles group)
Mary Nicholson
416 Chardonnay Drive
Fremont, CA 94539
(510) 490-4402

Bay Area Adoption Support
465 Fairchild Dr., Suite 215
Mountain View, CA 94043
(415) 964-3800

Inter Country Adoption Network (ICAN)
Jennifer Underwood
10419 Pearson Place
Sunland, CA 91040
(818) 352-0332

Colorado

Adoptive Families of Denver, Inc.
Violet Pierce
Box 3313
Littleton, CO 80161

Colorado Parents for All Children
Linda Donovan
780 E. Phillips Drive S.
Littleton, CO 80122
(303) 794-4838

Connecticut

Adoptive Parents Exchange Support Group
Deborah Stroffolino
6 Putnam Park Road
Bethel, CT 06801
(203) 743-9283

International Adoptive Families
Jeanne Allard
433 Quarry Brook Drive
South Windsor, CT 06074
(203) 644-0600

Delaware
Adoptive Families with Information & Support
Mary Lou Edgar
2610 Northgate Road
Wilmington, DE 19810
(302) 475-8925

District of Columbia
Barker Foundation Intl. Parents Group
Michelle Hester
4114 River Road NW
Washington, DC 20016
(202) 363-7751

North Virginia FACE
Eliza Button
103 15th Street, NE
Washington, DC 20002

Florida
Bay Area Adoptive Families
Dr. Kathie Erwin
305 Orangewood Lane
Largo, FL 34640
(813) 585-6010

Gatherings of Intl. Adoptive Families
Lori Stolt Bollman
2923 SW 5th Place
Cape Coral, FL 33914
(813) 574-4278

The Adoptive Resource Group
Grace Ahlsen-Girard
3006 Northwood Blvd.
Orlando, FL 32803
(407) 644-9627

Georgia

Adopted Kids and Parents Support Group
Marsha Kennedy
4137 Bellflower Court
Roswell, GA 30075
(404) 640-0031

Georgia Adoptive Parents, Inc.
Betty Lee Martin
1722 Wilmont Drive
Atlanta, GA 30329
(404) 325-4948

Hawaii

Adoptive Families of Kauai
Steve Soltysik
1702 Makoi Street
Lihue, Kauai, HI 96766
(808) 254-1711

Idaho

Adoptive Families of Southeastern Idaho
Beth McHugh
2356 Oak Trail Drive
Idaho Falls, ID 83404
(208) 529-3576

Families Involved in Adoption NW
DeeAnn Brennan
Box 612
Priest River, ID 83856
(208) 448-1779

Illinois

Chicago Area Families for Adoption
Jane Edmonds
Michael Mull
738 Nordic Court
Batavia, IL 60510
(708) 879-3125

International Families Through Adoption
Scott B. Johnson
3327 Lewis Drive
Quincy, IL 62301
(217) 224-3009

Indiana

Ours of Central Indiana
Randall and Suzetta Jenson
7920 Inverness Court
Indianapolis, IN 46237
(317) 888-9150

Tri-State Adoptive Families
Dan and Kathy Armstrong
8701 New Harmony Road
Evansville, IN 47721
(812) 963-6253

Iowa

Central Iowa Adoptive Families
Pam Millen
3740 Blanshan Drive
Ames, IA 50010
(515) 232-7872

Iowa City International Adoptive Families
Chris Forcucci
248 Hawkeye Court
Iowa City, IA 52246
(319) 353-5219

Kansas

International Families of Mid-America
Laura Hewitt
6708 Granada Road
Prairie Village, KS 66208
(913) 722-5697

Ours Through Adoption
Stacey M. Barnes
c/o Humana Hospital/Education Department
10500 Quivira
Overland Park, KS 66215
(913) 384-0459

Kentucky

Adoptive Parents Guild
Pamela Raidt
1888 Douglas Blvd.
Louisville, KY 40205
(502) 452-6578

Bluegrass Adoptive Parents' Support Group
Lorrie Mills
3319 Ridgecane Road
Lexington, KY 40513
(606) 224-3427

Louisiana

Catholic Social Services Auxiliary
Lynn Rogers
1106 Jenkins Street
Crowley, LA 70526
(318) 788-0431

Korean-American Resource Exchange
Gerri Lattier
8814 Bruin Road
Metairie, LA 70003
(504) 455-9445

Maine

Adoptive Families of Maine
Kitsie Claxton
129 Sunderland Drive
Auburn, ME 04210
(207) 784-3804

Maryland

Association of Single Adoptive Parents
Nancy Alexander
6718 Guide Avenue
Takoma Park, MD 20912
(301) 891-2084

Rainbow Families
Jim and Terri Cooney
128 East Lynbrook Place
Bel Air, MD 21014
(410) 838-3858

Massachusetts

Latin American Adoptive Families
Marilyn Rowland
40 Uplan Road
Duxbury, MA 02332
(617) 934-6756

Open Door Society of Massachusetts
Joan Clark
Box 1158
Westboro, MA 01581
(800) 932-3678

Michigan

Building Families Through Adoption
Alice Grogan
4874 Meyer Street
Cadillac, MI 49601
(616) 775-6202

European Adoptive Families of Southwest Michigan
Deborah Lawless
47540 Saltz Road
Canton, MI 48187
(313) 981-6534

Minnesota

OURS by Adoption
Cheryl Kalis
Box 7244
St. Cloud, MN 56302
(612) 356-7727

Parents of (Asian) Indian Children (PIC)
Lynn Mayfield
1395 Simpson Street
St. Paul, MN 55108
(612) 645-9068

Missouri

Families Through Adoption
Al and Chris Thimbur
1350 Summit Drive
Fenton, MO 63026
(314) 343-7658

International Families
Bob Henkel
15 N. Clay
St. Louis, MO 63134
(314) 423-6788

Montana

FACET, Inc.
Jeanne Scott
36th Street, N., #308
Great Falls, MT 59401
(406) 264-5590

Yellowstone International Adoptive Families
Joyce Evanson
4322 Stone
Billings, MT 59101
(406) 248-5157

Nebraska

Families Through Adoption
Lori Erickson
1619 Coventry Lane
Grand Island, NE 68801
(308) 381-8743

Parents of Adopted Children (PAC)
Jari Houston
16562 Ontario Circle
Omaha, NE 68135

New Hampshire

Open Door Society of New Hampshire
Betty and Gary Todd
40 Gerrish Drive
Nottingham, NH 03290
(603) 679-8144

New Jersey

Jersey Shore Families by Adoption
Anne Delli Sante
414 Washington Street
Toms River, NJ 08753
(908) 244-3694

Latin American Adoptive Parents Association
of North New Jersey, Inc.
Ruth Havens
170 Randolph Avenue
Dumont, NJ 07628
(201) 385-6278

New Mexico

Parents of InterCulture Adoptions, Inc.
Ann O'Rourke
Box 91175
Albuquerque, NM 87199
(505) 899-0457

New York

Adoptive Parents Committee-NY Chapter
Felix Fornino
Box 3525, Church Street Station
New York, NY 10008
(718) 259-7921

Families Interested in Adoption
L. and M. Kuenigsberg
Box 42
Buffalo, NY 14217-0042
(716) 649-6262

North Carolina

Carolina Adoptive Families
Kristen Blank
3200 Mill Pond Road
Charlotte, NC 28226
(704) 598-9632

Coastal Adoptive Families
Mary Roberts
2912 Colonial Lamb Road
Wilmington, NC 28405
(919) 350-0584

North Dakota

Adoption In Our Heart
Jan Kearns
2578 Willow Road, NE
Fargo, ND 58102
(701) 298-3052

The Adoption Forum
Kathy S. Rosario
1809 Country West Road
Bismarck, ND 58501
(701) 255-7720

Ohio

Adoptive Parent Support Organization
Jeff Stacy
2638 Ridgecliffe Avenue
Cincinnati, OH 45212
(513) 631-2883

Families Through Adoption
Jo Bennett
773 Cliffside Drive
Akron, Ohio 44313
(216) 869-2840

Oklahoma

Adoptive Parents of Northeast Oklahoma
Vince and Karen Griffin
2939 S. 95th East Avenue
Tulsa, OK 74129
(918) 665-7778

Families Helping Families
Betty Stout
Route 1, Box 58
Mead, OK 73449
(405) 920-0188

Oregon

Adoptive Families Unlimited
Diane Reinmuth
1061 Sharon Way
Eugene, OR 97401
(503) 345-5948

Northwest Adoptive Families Association, Inc.
Carol Bump
Box 25355
Portland, OR 97225

Pennsylvania

Adoption Forum
Abby Ruder
6808 Ridge Avenue
Philadelphia, PA 19128
(215) 487-1311

American Private Adoption Association
Trudy Grotzinger
Box 99235
Pittsburgh, PA 15233

Rhode Island

Adoption Rhode Island
Donna Caldwell
Box 1495
Kingston, RI 02881
(401) 792-3240

G.I.F.T. of R.I., Inc.
Lynn Sheridan
144 Old North Road
Kingston, RI 02881
(401) 789-2302

South Carolina

Piedmont Adoptive Families
Karen Kearse
Box 754
Spartanburg, SC 29304
(803) 578-3571

SC COAC
Lina Williams
1004 Sierra Drive
Easley, SC 29642
(803) 269-7713

South Dakota

Families Through Adoption
Diane Almos
218 18th Avenue, S.
Brookings, SD 57006
(605) 697-5806

Tennessee

Adopting Special Kids (ASK)
Cindy Pack
579 McAdoo Creek Road
Clarksville, TN 37043
(615) 358-3167

OURS of Middle Tennessee
Laura and Kent Madison
5104 Hickory Grove Drive
Antioch, TN 37013
(615) 641-2158

Texas

Adoptive Families Together
Joyce Gehring Zachmen
Box 272963
Houston, TX 77277-2963
(713) 980-4814

Council on Adoptable Children of Dallas
Bobbie T. Kerr
Box 141199, Dept. 366
Dallas, TX 75214
(214) 823-5047

Utah

Adoptive Support Group of Utah
Shauna Leishman
2835 S. Main
Salt Lake City, UT 84115
(801) 468-5493

Families Involved in Adoption (FIA)
Shelley Phillips
Box 746
Centerville, UT 84014
(801) 292-1062

Vermont

The Chosen Children from Romania
K. Mark Treon
Box 401
Barre, VT 05641
(802) 476-8063

Vermont Families Through Adoption
Judy LeMay
16 Aspen Drive
Essex Junction, VT 05452
(802) 878-1753

Virginia

Association of Single Adoptive Parents of Virginia
Vicky Bascom
408 Henry Clay Road
Ashland, VA 23005
(804) 798-2673

Families Through Adoption
Maryann Sparrow
1224 Wivenhoe Court
Virginia Beach, VA 23454

Washington

Adoptive Families Network of South Puget Sound
Karma Phillips
Box 112188
Tacoma, WA 98411-2188
(206) 565-6493

AIAA Adoptive Parent Support Group
Kristi Greene
S. 2711 Manito Blvd.
Spokane, WA 99203
(509) 624-2617

West Virginia

Appalachian Families for Adoption
Judy Dyer
Box 2275
Charleston, WV 25330

Parent Adoptive Link
Sandy Burkett
191 Ridgeway Drive
Bridgeport, WV 26330

Wisconsin

Adoptive Families Network
Jeanne Lewis
1939 Zimmerman Street
Wausau, WI 54401
(715) 845-9447

OURS of Greater Milwaukee
Mary Klein
6538 West Arch Avenue
Brown Deer, WI 53223
(415) 355-3970

Wyoming

Northern Wyoming Adoptive Parents, Inc.
Irene Tate
Box 788
Basin, WY 82410
(307) 568-2729

Northern Wyoming Adoptive Parents, Inc.
Pam Johnson
1298 Road 19 HC 73
Powell, WY 82410
(307) 754-5355

Parent-Group Magazines and Newsletters

Adopted Child
Lois R. Melina
P.O. Box 9362
Moscow, ID 83843
> Published monthly. $22.00/year; $38.00/two years.

The Adoption Advocate
Adoption Advocates International
136 Old Black Diamond Road
Port Angeles, WA 98362
> Published three times a year. $10.00/year.

Adoption Helper
189 Springdale Blvd.
Toronto Ontario
CANADA M4C 1Z6
(416) 463-9412
> Published quarterly. $25.00/year.

Adoption Today
WACAP
P.O. Box 88948
Seattle, WA 98138
> Published quarterly. Thirty-two pages of information on all aspects of adoption. $15.00/year.

The African Connection
Americans for African Adoption, Inc.
8910 Timberwood Drive
Indianapolis, IN 46234
> $20.00/year.

Buenas Noticias
Latin American Parents Association (LAPA)
P.O. Box 339
Brooklyn, NY 11234
(718) 236-8689

F.A.C.E. Facts
Families Adopting Children Everywhere
P.O. Box 28058, Northwood Station
Baltimore, MD 21239
(410) 488-2656
> Published bimonthly. Magazine and membership $20.00/year.

FAIR Newsletter
P.O. Box 51436
Palo Alto, CA 94303
> Published six times a year. Membership and newsletter $20.00/year.

ICCC Newsletter
911 Cyprus Drive
Boulder, CO 80303
> Published four times a year. $10.00 donation/year.

Los Ninos News
Los Ninos International
25231 Grogans Mill Road, #345
The Woodlands, TX 77380
> Monthly report on adoption situations, adoption stories, and pictures. Send a self-addressed, stamped envelope for a list of adoption-related books and videos. $24.00/year.

ODS News
Open Door Society of Massachusetts
P.O. Box 1158
Westborough, MA 01581-6158
(800) 93A-DOPT
> Published bimonthly. Contains all types of adoption information, including news on adoption seminars and conferences. $15.00/year.

OURS, The Magazine of Adoptive Families
Adoptive Families of America
3333 Highway 100 North
Minneapolis, MN 55422
(612) 535-4829
> Published bimonthly. Twice the winner of the Parent's Choice Foundation Gold Award. Highly recommended. $24.00/year; $42.00/two years; $58.00/three years.

Roots And Wings
P.O. Box 638
Chester, NJ 07930
(908) 852-8522
> Published quarterly. $20.00/year.

Stars of David
c/o Janie Allen
9 Hampton Street
Cranford, NJ 07016
> For Jewish adoptive families. $8.00/year.

Suggested Reading

The following books and booklets—about adoption, parenting, infertility, and other topics—should be available in your local bookstore. You can also order them. Request a catalog from one or more of these sources:

AFA, Attn: Parenting Resources
3333 Highway 100 N.
Minneapolis, MN 55422
(612) 535-4829; Fax: (612) 535-7808

Perspective Press
The Infertility and Adoption Publisher
P.O. Box 90318
Indianapolis, IN 46290

Tapestry Books
P.O. Box 359
Ringoes, NJ 08551
(800) 765-2367

Books about Adoption

Adamec, Christine A. *How to Adopt Your Baby Privately.* Adoption Advocates Press, 1992, 96 pages. This book is a guide to independent adoption through an attorney. The topics include how to find an attorney, what questions to ask, which birthmothers are least likely to change their minds, how to advertise, and how much the adoption will cost. This book lists 200 prominent adoption attorneys and how to contact them.

Adamec, Christine A. *There Are Babies to Adopt*. Bedford, MD: Mills and Sanderson, 1990, 352 pages. This book provides information you need for adoption, including listings of agencies, support groups, attorneys, and state laws.

Beauvais-Goodwin, Laura, and Raymond Godwin. *The Independent Adoption Manual*. Lakewood, NJ: Advocate Press, 1993, 395 pages. This book provides comprehensive information on the entire private adoption process. You will also find a detailed state-by-state guide of adoption laws.

Bolles, Edmund B. *The Penguin Adoption Handbook: A Guide to Creating Your Family*. New York, NY: Penguin, 1993, 256 pages. This is an updated guide to adopting a child. You will learn about the entire adoption process, adoption strategies, the process of finding a child, and adoption law.

Gilman, Lois. *Adoption Resource Book*. New York, NY: Harper & Row, 1992, 421 pages. This book takes you through the adoption process, teaches you how to prepare yourself for your child, and gives some guidelines for raising an adopted child. The book contains a resource section that lists adoption agencies (including agencies that do international adoption) and an annotated bibliography. This is a good book for prospective adoptive parents as well as for those who have already adopted.

Hicks, Randall B. *Adopting in America*. Sun City, CA: Word Slinger Press, 1993, 344 pages. A step-by-step guide to the adoption process. The book contains a comprehensive legal summary including adoption requirements, procedures, guidance for working with agencies and attorneys, necessary paperwork, waiting periods, and other topics. It is written by a prominent adoption attorney.

Martin, Cynthia. *Beating the Adoption Game*. San Francisco, CA: Oak Tree Publications, Harcourt Brace Jovanovich, 1988, 544 pages. This how-to guidebook shows the various options available in adoption today. It gives in-depth, practical advice to prospective adoptive parents. This book also provides you with valuable "tricks of the trade" to help you successfully complete your adoption.

Michelman, Stanley B. *The Private Adoption Handbook*. New York, NY: Villard Books, 1988, 220 pages. This reference book provides you with all the information you will need for adopting privately. It describes the steps of the process, explains how to choose an attorney, and provides examples of newspaper ads, parent résumés, and cover letters.

Walker, Elaine L. *Loving Journeys Guide to Adoption*. Peterboro, NH: Loving Journeys, 1992, 394 pages. This book gives a thorough introduction to the world of adoption, including the general requirements and procedures. It contains a directory of adoption resources such as private-adoption agencies, adoption attorneys, parent support groups, adoption programs, and international programs.

The Legal Aspects of Adoption

Adoption Laws: Answers to the Most Asked Questions. Rockville, MD: National Adoption Information Clearinghouse, updated. To order send ten dollars to the National Adoption Information Clearinghouse, Suite 410, 11426 Rockville Pike, Rockville, MD 20852. This excellent resource gives state-by-state answers to your legal questions. The book identifies who can adopt and who can be adopted, and discusses consent to adoption, the legal adoption process, the laws of confidentiality, permissible fees, location of the adoption hearing, authority to place the child, and adoption by relatives. It also describes the range of state variations.

Reference Books about Adoption

Adamec, Christine, and William L. Pierce, Ph.D. *The Encyclopedia of Adoption*. New York, NY: Facts on File, 1991, 419 pages. This reference book covers the social, legal, economic, psychological, and political issues that are related to the adoption experience. Nearly four hundred encyclopedia entries are indexed and cross-referenced. The many appendixes provide statistics and adoption organization information. This book is for both the parent and the professional.

Miles, Susan G. *Adoption Literature for Children and Young Adults*. Westport, CT: Greenwood Press, 1991, 232 pages. This book is an extensive annotated bibliography of the adoption literature for children and young adults published since 1900. The book describes five hundred nonfiction and fiction titles, covering books for the preschooler to the high schooler. It can be a valuable tool in helping you choose books on such varied topics as single-parent adoption, racial identity, and surrogacy.

Open Adoption

Rappaport, Bruce M., Ph.D. *The Open Adoption Book*. New York, NY: McMillian, 1992, 195 pages. This book gives an in-depth look at the process of open adoption and what it means. It will answer your questions as well as explain what you can expect emotionally.

Severson, Randolph, Ph.D. *A Letter to Adoptive Parents...
On Open Adoption.* Dallas, TX: House of Tomorrow, 1991,
28 pages. This booklet is an introduction to open adoption.
The author, a psychologist at an adoption agency, shares the
information he has found helpful to couples preparing for
open adoption.

Silber, Kathleen, and Phyllis Speedlin. *Dear Birthmother:
Thank You for Our Baby.* San Antonio, TX: Corona Publishing, 1991, 194 pages. This is the "classic" book on open
adoption. You will read actual letters written between members of adoptive families and birthparents. A caring and
compassionate look at openness in adoption, this book gives
practical advice and suggestions to help you consider open
adoption.

Parenting Resources

Adoptive Families of America (AFA)
3333 Highway 100 North
Minneapolis, MN 55422
(612) 535-4829; Fax: (612) 535-7808
     AFA, a nonprofit parent support organization, lists
more than 425 parenting resources in their bimonthly magazine, *Ours.* (Magazine and membership are $24.00/year,
$42.00/two years.) These invaluable resources include the
following:

- New adoption resources on the market
- Books on all aspects of adoption for children and adults
- Special-needs resources
- Multicultural resources, including books, multicultural
  dolls, and cookbooks
- Audiocassettes on various adoption and parenting issues

Adoption Benefits

Adoption Benefit Plans. National Adoption Exchange. For information write to National Adoption Exchange, 1218 Chestnut, Philadelphia, PA 19107.

International Adoption

Independent Adoption. Boulder, CO: ICCC, 1989. Send $2.50 to International Concerns Committee for Children, 911 Cypress Drive, Boulder, CO 80303.

Nelson-Erichsen, Jean, and Heino R. Erichsen. *How to Adopt Internationally.* The Woodlands, TX: Los Ninos International, 1992, 197 pages. This informative manual includes the latest information on international adoption sources and resources to help you complete an adoption in Africa, Asia, Europe, and Latin America. It contains adoption laws, procedures, and forms.

Parents Guide to Intercountry Adoption. Boston: Open Door Society of Massachusetts. Send $8.00 to Open Door Society of Massachusetts, 867 Boylston Street, 6th Floor, Boston, MA 02116.

Register, Cheri. *"Are Those Kids Yours?"* New York, NY: Free Press, 1991, 240 pages. This book will help you understand what is involved in becoming an international family, as well as why children are available for adoption in foreign countries. This book will also help you to know what to expect and what to say when strangers ask, "Are those kids yours?"

Report on Foreign Adoption. International Concerns Committee for Children. The most extensive and updated information available today on international adoption. A $20.00 annual donation includes ten updates. The ICCC also has a listing service that provides photos and descriptions of over five hundred available foreign-born children. A $25.00 annual donation includes ten updates. In addition, you can receive the quarterly ICCC Newsletter, which announces ICCC activities and discusses related topics, for an annual donation of $10.00. Write to ICCC, 911 Cypress Drive, Boulder, CO 80303.

Wirth, Eileen M. and Joan Worden, *How to Adopt a Child from Another Country*. Nashville: Abingdon Press. This book contains a good overview of adopting internationally, including true stories of two families. The book covers making the adoption decision to raising a foreign-born child.

Immigration and Naturalization Service (I.N.S.) District Offices

Alaska
New Federal Building
701 C. St., Room D229
Anchorage, AK 99513

Arizona
Federal Building
230 N. First Avenue
Phoenix, AZ 85025

California
300 N. Los Angeles Street
Los Angeles, CA 90012

880 Front Street
San Diego, CA 92188

Appraisers Building
630 Sansome Street
San Francisco, CA 94111

Colorado
1787 Federal Building
1961 Stout Street
Denver, CO 80294-1799

Florida
7880 Biscayne Blvd.
Miami, FL 33138

Georgia
Federal Annex Building
77 Forsyth Street SW
Room G-85
Atlanta, GA 30303

Hawaii
P.O. Box 461
595 Ala Moana Blvd.
Honolulu, HI 96809

Illinois
Dirksen Federal Office Building
219 S. Dearborn Street
Chicago, IL 60604

Louisiana
Postal Service Building
701 Loyola Avenue
New Orleans, LA 70113

Maine

739 Warren Avenue
Portland, ME 04103

Maryland

E. A. Garmatz Federal Building
101 W. Lombard
Baltimore, MD 21201

Massachusetts

JFK Federal Building
Government Center
Boston, MA 02203

Michigan

Federal Building
333 Mt. Elliot Street
Detroit, MI 48207

Minnesota

923 New P.O. Building
180 E. Kellogg Blvd.
St. Paul, MN 55101

Missouri

9747 N. Conant Avenue
Kansas City, MO 64153

Montana

Federal Building, Rm. 512
301 South Park
Drawer 10036
Helena, MT 59626-0036

New Jersey
Federal Building
970 Broad Street
Newark, NJ 07102

New York
68 Court Street
Buffalo, NY 14202

26 Federal Plaza
New York, NY 10278

Ohio
Anthony J. Celebreeze Federal Building,
Room 1917
1240 E. 9th Street
Cleveland, OH 44199

Oregon
Federal Office Building
511 NW Broadway
Portland, OR 92709

Pennsylvania
1600 Callowhill Street
Philadelphia, PA 19103

Texas
Rm. 6A21, Federal Building
1100 Commerce Street
Dallas, TX 75242

511 E. San Antonio
Room 151
El Paso, TX 79984

2102 Teege Avenue
Harlingen, TX 78550

509 N. Belt
Houston, TX 77060

Federal Building, Suite A301
727 E. Durango
San Antonio, TX 78206

Washington
Airport Way, S.
Seattle, WA 98134

Washington, DC
4420 N. Fairfax Drive
Arlington, VA 22203

Puerto Rico
GPO Box 5068
San Juan, PR 00936

Single-Parent Adoption

Curto, Josephine J. *How to Become a Single Parent: A Guide for Single People Considering Adoption or Natural Parenthood Alone.* Englewood Cliffs, NJ: Prentice-Hall, 1983.

Marindin, Hope. *The Handbook for Single Adoptive Parents.* Chevy Chase, MD: Committee for Single Adoptive Parents, 1992. Write to Committee for Single Adoptive Parents, P.O. Box 15084, Chevy Chase, MD 20825.

Single Parents with Adopted Kids. This is the only national newsletter for singles who have adopted. Write to Dannette Kaslow-SWAK, 4108 Washington Rd., #101, Kenosha, WI 53144 for information. The newsletter costs twenty dollars per year for four issues.

Raising Adopted Children

Bothun, Linda. *When Friends Ask About Adoption.* Houston, TX: Swan Publications, 1987, 88 pages. This informative question-and-answer-guide will answer the adoption questions of grandparents, relatives, teachers, neighbors, and friends, as well as show them how to be supportive of the adoptive family.

Melina, Lois R. *Making Sense of Adoption: A Parent's Guide.* New York, NY: Harper-Collins, 1989, 256 pages. This book offers advice about how you can help your child deal with the issue of adoption at various stages of development. Each chapter suggests age-specific activities that you can use to help your child with various adoption concepts. The book includes some sample conversations that can guide you as you talk to your child.

Melina, Lois R. *Raising Adopted Children.* New York, NY: Harper-Collins, 1986, 288 pages. This guide is a "must" for adoptive parents. It examines the adopted child's physical, emotional, and psychological development at every age. This book also covers multiracial families, behavior problems, and single-parent adoption.

Smith, Dorothy W., and Laurie N. Sherwen. *Mothers and Their Adopted Children: The Bonding Process.* New York, NY: Tiresias Press, 1988, 208 pages. This book is good for parents who wonder or worry about the bonding process in adoption. This book looks at the emotional aspects of the parent-child relationship in adoption. It also discusses open records, the identity of the adopted child, and the emotional aspects of the racially or ethnically different child during adolescence.

Audiotapes, Music Resources, and Videotapes on Adoption

Audiotapes

The Catalog of Audiovisual Materials can be ordered from the National Adoption Information Clearinghouse, Suite 410, 11426 Rockville Pike, Rockville, MD 20852, (301) 231-6512.

The following audiocassettes are available from Adopted Child, P.O. Box 9362, Moscow, ID 83843, (208) 882-1794.

Introduction to Adoption for Family and Friends, 60 minutes, 1990. This tape is recommended for grandparents-to-be. It provides an overview of adoption issues, with an emphasis on the grief that extended family members may feel when a relative is infertile or when a relative adopts. $8.95.

The Joys and Challenges of Raising Adopted Children, 60 minutes, 1990. This tape discusses how losses connected with adoption affect infertile and fertile parents and how they provide opportunities for family growth. $8.95.

While You Wait to Adopt, 60 minutes, 1991. This tape discusses how adoptive-parents-to-be can prepare physically and psychologically for their transition to parenthood. $8.95.

Music Resources

Music for Little People is a company that offers musical instruments, tapes, books, and records from many cultures. Contact them at Box 1460, Redway, CA 95560, 1-800-346-4445.

World Music Press offers a catalog of songbooks, sheet music, resource books, audiocassettes, and videotapes from around the world. They can be reached at Box 2565, Danbury, CT 06813, (203) 748-1131.

Videotapes

The following videotapes are available from AdopTapes, 4012 Lynn Avenue, Edina, MN 55416, (612) 922-1136.

Birthparents Speak about Adoption, 40 minutes, $29.95.

A Candid Talk about Loss in Adoption, 1 hour, $35.95.

So You're Going to Adopt?, VHS; 41 minutes, 1989. This video speaks about the realities of adoption, including infertility, raising adopted children, and nurturing one's marital relationship before and after the adoption. $29.95 plus $3.50 shipping and handling.

The following videotapes can be ordered from Start To Finish Video, 2270 St. Clair, St. Paul, MN 55105.

Full Circle: The Korean Journey is the story of a mother who travels to Korea to pick up her new child. You will follow her as she visits the adoption agency, an infant's reception center, a pediatric hospital, a home for unwed mothers, and a foster home. Some Korean adoption workers give their insights into the adoption process of Korean infants. $19.95 plus $3.00 shipping and handling. (Minnesota residents add 6.5 percent sales tax.)

The Long Journey Home is the story of Katie and her new American family. This is a factual depiction of the adoption of a Korean-born infant.

The following videos are available from Hope Cottage Adoption Center, 4209 McKinney Avenue, Suite 200, Dallas, TX 75205, (214) 526-8721.

> *The Gift: A Video about and for Adoption*, 24 minutes. This award-winning film captures the delicate and volatile emotions of a sixteen-year-old girl on her birthday as she struggles, along with her parents, to come to terms with both the mystery and the meaning of adoption. $23.95 including shipping and handling.

> *House of Tomorrow*, VHS, 12 minutes, 1990. A refreshing look at the open adoption process. The video includes a unique adoption ceremony. $19.00 including shipping and handling.

> *Talking with Your Child about Adoption*, VHS. This video will help you talk openly with your child about adoption. Topics include understanding adoption at various ages, preparing your child for school and for dealing with the outside world on adoption, adoption rituals and celebrations, and adoption terminology. $19.00 including shipping and handling.

Adoption: Your Guide to Success, VHS, 70 minutes, 1990. This is a tape aimed at prospective adoptive parents. It discusses infant and special needs and intercountry, independent, and agency adoption as well as open and closed adoption. KCET Video, 4401 Sunset Blvd., Los Angeles, CA 90027, 1-800-765-7890. $39.95 plus $3.50 shipping and handling.

Families with Special Needs Children, multimedia. Contains workbooks, leaders' guides, filmstrips, and tapes to educate the public about raising children with special needs. It is useful for those who are considering the adoption of a special-needs child. Funded by the March of Dimes Birth Defects Foundation and available from Educational Development Center, 55 Chapel Sreet, Newton, MA 02160, (617) 969-7100.

Special-Needs Adoption

Batshaw, Mark, and Yvonne Perret. *Children with Handicaps.* Baltimore, MD: Paul H. Brookes Publishing, 1988.

Dorris, Michael. *The Broken Cord.* New York, NY: Harper-Collins, 1989, 300 pages. This book won the 1989 National Book Critics Circle Award for nonfiction. In 1992 it was made into a TV movie. This book is a true account of a father coming to terms with his adopted son's fetal alcohol syndrome. This is a good book for anyone considering adopting a child with a family history of alcohol or substance abuse.

McNamara, Joan, and Bernard McNamara, eds. *Adoption and the Sexually Abused Child.* Family Resources, 1990, 203 pages. Estimates show that approximately 75 percent of children waiting for adoption in the U.S. have been sexually abused. This book covers the many issues that a parent may face in adopting an older and/or waiting child, and it discusses some ways to handle those issues.

Pueschel, Siegfried, James Bernier, and Leslie Bernier. *The Special Child.* Baltimore, MD: Paul H. Brooks Publishing, 1988.

Severson, Randolph W. *Can't You Sit Still? Adoption and Attention Deficit Hyperactivity Disorder.* Wearerville, CA: House of Tomorrow, 70 pages. This book is written specifically as a message of hope for adoptive parents. It gives practical advice, including suggestions for behavior management, and discusses such related topics as Ritalin and diet.

Turecki, Stanley, M.D., and Leslie Tonner. *The Difficult Child.* New York, NY: Phantom, 1985, 224 pages. This book closely examines the behaviors of "hard to raise" children. It provides a detailed approach to living with a difficult child.

Special-Needs Children: Sources for Information and Support

National Associations

Alliance of Genetic Support Groups
38th & R Streets, NW
Washington, DC 20057
(202) 331-0942

Association for Retarded Citizens
2501 Avenue J
Arlington, TX
(817) 588-2000

Cystic Fibrosis Foundation
6931 Arlington Road
Bethesda, MD 20814
(301) 951-4422

Epilepsy Foundation of America
4351 Garden City Drive
Landover, MD 20785
(301) 459-3700

March of Dimes Birth Defects Foundation
1275 Mamaroneck Avenue
White Plains, NY 10605
(914) 428-7100

Muscular Dystrophy Association
3561 East Sunrise Drive
Tucson, AZ 85718
(602) 529-2000

National Down's Syndrome Congress
1800 Dempster Street
Park Ridge, IL 60068
(708) 823-7550

National Association for Perinatal Addiction
Research and Education
11 East Hubbard Street, Suite 200
Chicago, IL 60611
(312) 329-2512

National Easter Seal Society
70 East Lake Street
Chicago, IL 60601
(312) 726-6200

National Society for Autistic Children
1234 Massachusetts Avenue, NW, Suite 1017
Washington, DC 20005-4599
(202) 783-0125

Spina Bifida Association
1770 Rockville Pike, Suite 540
Rockville, MD 20852
(800) 621-3141

United Cerebral Palsy Association
7 Penn Plaza, Suite 804
New York, NY 10001
(212) 268-6655

Clearinghouse and Government Information

ATTN: Development Disabilities
Department of Health and Human Services
Office of Human Development Services
200 Independence Avenue, SW, HHH Building
Room 336D
Washington, DC 20201
(202) 245-1961

International Special Olympics
1350 New York Avenue, NW
Washington, DC 20005
(202) 628-3630

National Information Center for Handicapped
    Children and Youth
P.O. Box 1492
Washington, DC 20013
(703) 893-6061

National Resource Center for Special Needs Adoption
17390 W. Eight Mile Road
Southfield, MI 48075
(313) 443-0300

Adoption Exchanges

The CAP Book (Children Waiting for Adoptive Parents)
700 Exchange Street
Rochester, NY 14608
(716) 232-5110

National Adoption Exchange
1218 Chestnut Street
Philadelphia, PA 19107
(215) 925-0200

Medical Information

The Mayo Clinic Family Health Book provides reliable, practical, comprehensive, and easy-to-understand information on issues relating to good health. Much of this book's information comes directly from the experience of the clinic's eleven hundred physicians and research scientists. The book supplements the advice of your personal physician, whom you should consult for individual medical problems. *The Mayo Clinic Family Health Book* does not endorse any company or product.

Larson, David E., *Mayo Clinic Family Health Book*, New York: William Morrow and Company, Inc., 1990. ISBN 0-688-07819-2.

Peter, George, ed., *Report on the Committee on Infectious Diseases*, 22nd edition, 1991.

American Academy of Pediatrics
141 Northwest Point Blvd.
P.O. Box 927
Elk Grove Village, IL 60009-0927
ISBN 0-919761-27-2

BIBLIOGRAPHY

Adamec, Christine. *There Are Babies to Adopt: A Resource Guide for Prospective Parents*. Bedford, MA: Mills and Sanderson, 1987.

Adoptive Families of America. *Ours* Magazine, AFA, (January-June 1993).

Finnegan, Loretta P., M.D., and Bonnie A. MacNew, R.N., B.S.N., eds. "Care of the Addicted Infant." *American Journal of Nursing*, 74, 4 (April 1974): 685-692. A comprehensive discussion of the problems that may beset the baby born to the narcotic-dependent mother, and recommendations for their solution.

Gilman, Lois. *The Adoption Resource Book*. New York: Harper & Row, 1990.

"Grolier Electronic: Prodigy." *Academic American Encyclopedia*. Danbury, CT: Grolier Inc., 1993.

I.N.S. *The Immigration of Adopted and Prospective Adoptive Children*. Washington, DC: Superintendent of Documents, 1990.

International Concerns Committee for Children. *Report on Foreign Adoption*, Boulder, CO: ICCC, 1992.

Larson, David E., M.D., ed. *The Mayo Clinic Family Health Book*. New York: William Morrow and Company, 1990.

Lowry, Lynn. "Confronting Obstacles in the Adoption Process, Going It Alone: The Challenge of Single Parenting," *Ours* Magazine, 26, 1 (January-February 1993).

Magers, Linda. "Children with Attention Deficit Disorder," *Ours* Magazine, 26, 2 (March-April 1993).

Marindin, Hope. *The Handbook for Single Adoptive Parents*. Chevy Chase, MD: Committee for Single Adoptive Parents, 1992.

Martin, Cynthia. *Beating the Adoption Game*. San Diego, CA: Harcourt Brace Jovanovich, 1988.

McNamara, Joan, M.S. "The Realities of Adopting an Older Child," *Ours* Magazine, 26, 2 (March-April 1993).

Melina, Lois. *Adoption: An Annotated Bibliography and Guide*. New York: Garland Publishing, 1987.

Michelman, Stanley. *The Private Adoption Handbook: A Step-by-Step Guide to the Legal, Emotional and Practical Demands of Adopting a Baby*. New York: Villard Books, 1988.

Mizgerd, Joseph B., M.D. *The Lippincott Manual of Nursing Practice*. Philadelphia: J. B. Lippincott, 1981.

National Adoption Information Clearinghouse. *Adoption Laws: Answers to the Most Asked Questions.* Rockville, MD: NAIC, 1993.

National Committee for Adoption: *The Adoption Fact Book.* NCA, 1989.

Nelson-Erichsen, Jean and Heino R. Erichsen. *How to Adopt Internationally: A Guide for Agency Directed and Independent Adoptions.* The Woodlands, TX: Los Ninos International, 1992.

Plotkin, Stanley, M.D., Chairman of the Committee on Infectious Diseases. "Report on the Committee on Infectious Diseases." 22nd ed. Elk Grove Village, IL: American Academy of Pediatrics, 1991.

Posner, Julia. *The Adoption Resource Guide.* Washington, DC: Child Welfare League of America, 1990.

Samuels, Shirley. *Ideal Adoption: A Comprehensive Guide to Forming an Adoptive Family.* New York: Plenum Press, 1990.

Scipien, Gladys M. *Comprehensive Pediatric Nursing.* New York: McGraw-Hill, 1979.

Shaywitz, Sally E., M.D. "Devising the Proper Drug Therapy for Attention Deficit Disorders." *Contemporary Pediatrics,* 1 (October 1984).

Vincent, Judith. "Finding an Adoption Attorney," *Ours Magazine,* 26, 1 (January-February 1993).

INDEX

About the Authors

Connie Crain is a registered nurse who has spent the past eight years working in the labor and delivery/ maternal child care unit of a small community hospital. She and her husband have one adopted daughter and are in the process of adopting another child. She enjoys traveling, reading, and entertaining friends.

Janice Duffy grew up in East Africa as the daughter of foreign missionaries. She received her B.S. in Nursing from Samford University in Birmingham, Alabama. Janice has spent her nursing career working in the Neonatal Intensive Care field. She and her husband have five children. Her two youngest daughters were adopted from Romania. When Janice is not writing, she enjoys hunting for antiques, traveling, and swimming.